INDIA,

ITS

STATE AND PROSPECTS

INDIA,

ITS

STATE AND PROSPECTS.

EDWARD THORNTON, Esq.

GYAN

Published by

Gyan Publishing House
5, Ansari Road
Daryaganj, New Delhi-110002
Phone: 011-47034999, 9811692060
E-mail: books@gyanbooks.com

Distribution Network
gyanbooks.com
India, USA, Canada, UK, Australia, France

ISBN: 978-81-212-8692-3 (PB)
First Published, 1835

2nd Impression 2023

Printed at: Gyan Press, Delhi.

INDIA, ITS STATE AND PROSPECTS
Author: Edward Thornton

INDIA,

ITS

STATE AND PROSPECTS.

INDIA,

ITS

STATE AND PROSPECTS.

BY

EDWARD THORNTON, Esq.

LONDON:
PARBURY, ALLEN, & CO.,
LEADENHALL STREET.

1835.

PREFACE.

THE Act which last year passed the British Legislature, "for effecting an Arrangement with the East-India Company, and for the better Government of His Majesty's Indian Territories," has created an era in the history of those territories; and seems to afford a fitting opportunity for taking a view of their situation and resources. Such an attempt can scarcely be regarded as unnecessary when it is recollected, that the majority even of the best-informed of our countrymen are either entirely ignorant of the subject, or but superficially acquainted with it. Neither our long intercourse with India, nor the splendour of our commerce and our conquests there—neither the intrinsic importance of the subject, nor the repeated and animated discussions which it has excited in the British Parliament; have secured for it that degree of popular attention which it deserves. Statesmen of eminent name have observed and lamented this fact, which, considering the intense interest which has been taken in matters little less remote, and certainly not of greater importance, appears both inconsistent and inexplicable. Whether the opening a large part of India to European adventure will have the effect of dispelling this apathy, remains to be seen. That it is not justified by the relative circumstances of India and England is the conviction of the author. Under this conviction, he has been desirous of drawing attention to a subject which he feels to have been unduly neglected; and he has thought that a popular view of the state and prospects of British India might afford the best means of attaining his object. To this it has been deemed expedient to prefix a very brief Historical Sketch. It is true that histories of India, both learned and popular, are not wanting; but a very short summary of the principal facts of the progress of our extraordinary dominion seemed indispensable. The reader however who feels the importance and interest of the subject, will not be satisfied with a few pages; he will apply to works of greater extent and more strictly historical character to gratify a curiosity which it is hoped may here be excited.

Of the rest of the work the author trusts that he may speak with greater confidence. On the political relations of India—on the mode of its government—on the sources of its wealth and prosperity—on the state of society, manners, religion, and morals—on its judicial system, and the revenue which not only supports the national institutions, but remits to this country a noble tribute, little is known because the sources of knowledge have been generally inaccessible. Much information was scattered about, but it was nowhere collected within a moderate space. The changes effected by the late Act are now first brought before the Public in a permanent form; and the work, notwithstanding its limited extent, may be regarded as containing a digest of the most important parts of the vast body of evidence submitted to Parliament previously to the passing of that Act.

Though the circumstances of the times have induced him to choose this period for publication, they have had no share in determining the course of the author's inquiries. India has long occupied the larger share of his time and attention. To promote her interests as well as those of his own country, is the object of his work, and if an exposition of her resources should tend to draw British capital to their development, he believes that both nations would be benefited. On the important subject of religion, he trusts that he has acquitted himself with charity as well as zeal; and if an author may in any way be permitted to offer an opinion on his own labour, he would say that the chapter on the Judicial System contains some original disquisitions, the subjects of which, at least, are important; and that on the Revenue presents a somewhat comprehensive view of the various systems founded on the best authorities, and fortified by the opinions of the most eminent statesmen.

CONTENTS.

CHAPTER I.

HISTORICAL SKETCH.

Chapter II.

POLITICAL SKETCH.

Chapter III.

GOVERNMENT OF INDIA.

Power

CHAPTER IV.

AGRICULTURE.

Chapter V.

MANUFACTURES.

Chapter VI.

FOREIGN TRADE.

Chapter VII.

PUBLIC WORKS—MEANS OF FOREIGN AND INTERNAL COMMUNICATION.

Chapter VIII.

SOCIETY AND MANNERS.

Chapter IX.

RELIGION AND MORALS.

ill

CHAPTER X.

THE JUDICIAL SYSTEM.

Primary

Chapter XI.

REVENUE.

venue

CHAPTER XII.

MEANS OF SECURING BRITISH INTERESTS AND AUTHORITY.

INDIA,

&c. &c.

CHAPTER I.

HISTORICAL SKETCH.

THE early history of India is involved in extreme obscurity, and fable has in consequence usurped the place of fact. The ridiculous fictions which the Hindoos dignify with the name of history are unworthy not only of belief, but even of grave consideration. Little of either pleasure or information would be afforded by a detailed account of the solar and lunar dynasties, or an investigation of the accuracy of chronicles which carry us back through countless ages. Our best information is derived from the Greeks; and until the conquests of Alexander, they were acquainted with India only through vague and meagre reports obtained from the Persians. Alexander passed the different rivers of the Punjaub, and advanced towards the Ganges, which, however, he was not destined to reach. The narratives of his followers are admitted to be, in some

respects,

respects, discordant; and though previous to the time of Ptolemy the spirit of commercial adventure had added something to the stock of information, the knowledge of India possessed by the Greeks must be regarded as both scanty and inaccurate; but though unsatisfactory, it is sufficient to shew that the people to whom it relates are almost unchanged by the lapse of centuries. Even the minute features of the national character are at this time the same that they were two thousand years ago.

Though capable of being trained into efficient soldiers, the natives of India have not been fortunate in maintaining their independence, and they have generally afforded an easy triumph to a bold and determined invader. A large portion of their country was subject to the Persian monarchy; to Alexander they offered some resistance, but his conquests were effected in no long space of time; and at a later period they became, first tributaries, and ultimately subjects of the victorious disciples of Mahomet.

Previously to the invasion of the Moguls, the Mahometan history of India possesses slender interest, and is, perhaps, little to be relied on. For a considerable time after that event, it offers but a picture of those commotions and crimes which characterize a state of society in which conflicting parties are struggling for the sovereignty. The most

most remarkable person of this period was Timur, or Tamerlane; a man who, though exhibited by an English poet as a model of clemency, as well as of heroism, had little pretension to the former quality. His conquests extended from the Irtisch and Volga to the Persian Gulph, and from the Ganges to the Archipelago. He even meditated the invasion of China, and had made vast preparations for an expedition against that country, when death intercepted his career. His courage, perseverance, and military skill are indisputable; but, unfortunately, his cruelty is not less so.

The death of Timur took place about ninety years before the arrival of the Portuguese in India by the south-east passage, the discovery of which was to effect a revolution in the destinies of the country, compared with which all previous changes were unimportant. The great mass of commerce between India and Europe was carried on by the route of the Red Sea until the seventh century, when the conquest of Egypt by the Saracens transferred it by the Black Sea to Constantinople. When, however, the Mamelukes became masters of Egypt, they permitted the Venetians to resume the ancient route; and Alexandria was thenceforward the sole entrepôt of Indian trade.

The spirit of Portuguese discovery received its impulse from the genius of Prince Henry, youngest

est son of John I. of Portugal. Under his countenance naval adventure became popular; but the progress of discovery was greatly impeded by the imperfect state of navigation. The first acquisition was but of small importance, consisting only of the little island of Puerto Santo. It was sufficient, however, to encourage confidence, and stimulate to further exertions, and a subsequent expedition was rewarded by the discovery of the rich and beautiful island of Madeira.

After a tedious succession of voyages continued for nearly half a century, Vasco de Gama, an active and enterprizing Portuguese admiral, doubled the Cape of Good Hope, and coasting along the eastern shore of the continent of Africa, sailed from thence across the Indian Ocean, and landed at Calicut on the coast of Malabar. At the period of his arrival the west coast of Hindostan was divided between two great sovereigns, the king of Cambay and the Zamorin, each of whom had under him numerous petty princes. The dominions of the Zamorin included the whole coast from Bombay to Cape Comorin; but the attempts of De Gama to conclude a commercial treaty with this power were frustrated by the jealousy of the Mahometan merchants, and he returned to Lisbon. His successor, Cabral, was not more fortunate, and in consequence he proceeded to Cochin and Cananore. The kings of these

these places were dependents upon the Zamorin: a dependency from which they were anxious to be emancipated. By them Cabral was very favourably received; and in an incredibly short time the Portuguese acquired a paramount influence over the whole coast. Previously, however, to the arrival of Albuquerque in 1508, they were not possessed of a good port. After a violent struggle they secured and fortified Goa, which from thenceforth became the capital of the Portuguese settlements, and the point from whence they spread their conquests and their commerce over the Eastern seas.

The Venetians and the sultan of Egypt, who were the principal sufferers by the diversion of the commerce of the east into a new channel, made some ineffectual attempts, in conjunction with the king of Cambay, to dispossess the Portuguese of their conquests; but the latter not only maintained their superiority, but succeeded in acquiring the command of the Red Sea and the Persian Gulf. The trade by those routes consequently ceased, and feeling secure from competition, the Portuguese proceeded to push their success. In the course of a few years they established a commercial empire of unprecedented extent, splendour, and opulence; they commanded the east coast of Africa, the coasts of Arabia and Persia, the two peninsulas of India, the Moluccas, Ceylon, and the

the trade to China and Japan. They levied tribute upon a hundred and fifty native princes, and claimed a right to sweep from the Indian seas every vessel that sailed without their permission. Of all this mighty dominion, a miserable remnant is all that now exists, and that remnant depressed, impoverished, and almost in a state of estrangement from the mother country.

The annexation of Portugal to the crown of Spain was fatal to the colonial dominion of the former country, and the Dutch occupy the next conspicuous place in the commercial history of India. They had originally been contented with the carrying trade between Lisbon and the north of Europe; but Philip II. having put an end to this trade, they endeavoured to repair their loss by the discovery of a passage to India by the northward. Failing in this attempt, they embraced the proposal of Hautman, a prisoner for debt at Lisbon, to reveal to them the knowledge he possessed of Indian navigation and commerce on condition of his liberation. Four ships were dispatched to India under the command of Hautman in the year 1594, and a sanguinary war with the Portuguese soon followed. Success was long doubtful; but the Dutch ultimately triumphed. The Portuguese at first lost Malacca and Ceylon; they were subsequently driven from various settlements on the coast of Malabar; and not long afterwards

afterwards the native princes permitted the Dutch to establish factories at Negapatam, Sadras, Pulicat, and Bimlipatam, on the east coast. From this period the power of Portugal in the east was rapidly approaching to extinction.

The spirit of rivalry to the Portuguese was not confined to the Dutch. The splendid results which had followed the discovery of the south-east passage could scarcely fail to excite the emulation of a maritime and enterprising nation like the English. Two attempts were made in the reign of Henry VIII. to explore a north-west passage, and one in the reign of Edward VI. to discover a passage by the north-east. Many similar attempts followed within a short space of time, but all with the same want of success. There seemed, therefore, no alternative but to renounce the glittering visions of oriental wealth, or to follow them in the same track which the Portuguese had so successfully pursued. The first attempt to proceed by the south-east was however unprosperous. After encountering some Spanish men-of-war on the coast of Brazil, the expedition was obliged to return for want of provisions. The second expedition was still more unfortunate; the ships, three in number, were driven on the coast of Spanish America, and the crews, with the exception of four men, perished.

The more fortunate expeditions of Drake and Cavendish,

Cavendish, and their flattering reports of the wealth of the countries which they had visited, kept alive the national ardour for a participation in the Indian trade, and the fact of the Dutch having resolved on contending with the Portuguese for a share of this coveted traffic, determined the English to follow their example. An association was formed and a fund subscribed for the purpose, and a memorial presented to the Government, setting forth the places with which the Spanish and Portuguese had established intercourse, and pointing out others to which the English might resort without affording ground of complaint to their predecessors. Some difficulties were interposed by the Government on account of a treaty then pending with Spain, but permission was given to make preparations for a voyage, while the patent of incorporation was under consideration. The Government of the day appears to have been not indisposed to share in the patronage created by the adventure, and recommended Sir Edward Mitchelbourne to be employed in the expedition. The answer of the Directors affords a memorable proof of their independence, and must be regarded as peculiarly honourable to them, when it is considered that they were at the time petitioners to the throne for a charter. On consultation they resolved "not to employ any *gen-* "*tleman* in any place of charge, and requested "that

"that they might be allowed to sorte theire "business with men of theire own qualitye, lest "the suspiceon of the employmt of gentlemen "being taken hold upon by the generalitie, do "dryve a greate number of the adventurers to "withdraw their contributions."

Greatly to the honour of the Government, the honest resistance offered to its interference was not permitted to prejudice the cause of the adventurers, and on the last day of the year 1600, they were by letters-patent from the Queen constituted a body politic and corporate, by the title of "the Governor and Company of Merchants of London trading to the East-Indies." The government of the Company was vested in a committee of twenty-four and a chairman. It was empowered to trade to all places beyond the Cape of Good Hope and the Straits of Magellan for fifteen years, with the exception of places in possession of princes in amity with the Queen, whose objection should be publicly declared; and all other the Queen's subjects were prohibited from interfering with the Company's exclusive trade, except by license granted under their common seal. From James I. a renewal of the charter was obtained, by which all preceding privileges of the Company were confirmed, and they were constituted a body corporate for ever.

The early voyages of the Company were confined

fined to the islands of the Indian Ocean; but after the confirmation and extension of their charter by James they proceeded to establish a commercial intercourse with the Asiatic continent. Their endeavours were of course opposed by the Portuguese; but the English Company finally succeeded in establishing factories on various parts of the coast. One of their earliest settlements was at Surat, and this factory with that at Bantam remained for a long period their principal stations.

In the Dutch, the English Company found enemies more formidable than the Portuguese. The Dutch were bent on securing a monopoly of the spice trade, and they enforced it in the most unscrupulous and vindictive spirit. After a long course of hostility, relieved by some weak and inefficient attempts at pacification, the spirit of the whole British people, with the exception of their pusillanimous sovereign, was roused to the highest pitch of indignation by the atrocious proceedings at Amboyna. The Dutch, having determined on obtaining the exclusive possession of the island, fabricated a plot to afford them a pretext for effecting their purpose. The plot, it was pretended, was confessed by two soldiers in the Dutch service, one a Japanese, the other a Portuguese, who had been put to the torture. Upon this evidence the English were apprehended, imprisoned, loaded with irons, and their books

and

and property seized. A mock trial followed, in the course of which the prisoners were subjected to the most varied and horrible tortures, for the purpose of extorting confession. It is unnecessary to say that this mode of examination was successful. There is a point where human firmness must yield : the love of truth and the consciousness of innocence may sustain the sufferer for a time, but these motives will be overcome by protracted agony. Had the victims of the Dutch been accused of conspiring against the crown of England, the result would have been the same; they would have purchased remission of pain by the acknowledgment of guilt. Confession was of course followed by conviction—conviction by execution—and the commercial interests of the Dutch were cemented by the blood of the accused persons. A modern historian of India has chosen to take his post with the enemies of his country, and to employ much ingenuity in extenuating the guilt of the Dutch. But the atrocity admits not of palliation. The pretence of a conspiracy was too absurd to deceive even the most credulous. When the boxes of the factors were opened and their papers rifled, no traces of such conspiracy were discovered. The number of English on the island did not exceed twenty, while the Dutch had a garrison of three hundred men in the fort and several other garrisons in the island. The

English

English were not only few in number, but they were unprovided with arms and ammunition. They had not a single ship, whereas the Dutch had eight lying off the town of Amboyna. A conspiracy against the Dutch authorities, under such circumstances, could have been formed only by men labouring under insanity; and those who professed to believe in its existence, had they been sincere, would have justly fallen under the same imputation. The pen of the historian should not be employed in opposition to the interests of justice and humanity: and it is no less painful than astonishing to find an able writer of the nineteenth century taxing his abilities to justify conduct so horrible as that of the Dutch in this transaction, and even to excuse the application of torture as an instrument for the investigation of truth. It would be idle to say a word in refutation of a mode of trial from which common sense and humanity alike recoil. The torture procured for the Dutch authorities that which they wanted—a legal excuse for the condemnation of their victims; but the courage of the sufferers revived as they approached a more righteous tribunal, and on the awful verge of eternity they solemnly protested their innocence.

Those who will deliberately commit the graver crime of murder, will of course not hesitate at the comparatively light one of robbery. Massacre

was

was not unnaturally followed by confiscation, and the Dutch retained English property to an immense amount. Its value has been stated at £400,000. The truckling policy of James deterred him from seeking reparation of this great national wrong, and the disturbed reign of Charles allowed the Dutch a prolonged period of impunity; but the honour of the country was in some degree vindicated by Oliver Cromwell, who required and obtained payment of a large sum in satisfaction of the pecuniary injury inflicted.

At this time all the factories in the tract extending from Cape Comorin to the Persian and Arabian Gulphs were controlled by the presidency of Surat. On the coast of Coromandel the Company had established themselves in the first instance at Masulipatam. Subsequently they left that place for Armegum. Finally they settled at Madraspatam, where, by permission of the Native Government, they erected Fort St. George, now the seat of one of the British presidencies.

The connexions of the Company with Bengal were formed gradually. The first privilege which they obtained from the court of Delhi was that of free resort to the port of Pipley, a privilege afterwards much extended, through the intervention of a surgeon named Boughton, who acquired influence at the imperial court by the exercise of his professional skill. Factories were accordingly established

established at Hooghley, Cossimbazar, Balasore, Patna, and Malda. Of these Hooghley was chief, but the whole of them were subordinate to Fort St. George.

The accession of Charles II. to the throne was followed by a renewal of the charter of the Company, by which their ancient privileges were confirmed, and authority conveyed to them to make peace and war with any people, not being Christians, and to seize unlicensed persons within their limits, and send them to England. From the same prince they obtained a grant of the island of Bombay, which he had received as part of the marriage portion of Catherine of Portugal. This island, now the seat of a presidency, was on its first acquisition subordinate to Surat.

Though the British interest in India was on the whole progressive, its advance was not uninterrupted. A civil war in Bantam was the means of excluding the English from that part of India, while the factories of Surat and Bombay were disturbed by unremitting war between the Mogul and the Mahrattas. The Mogul empire was established by Baber, a descendant of Timur, already mentioned, and sultan of the Mogul Tartars. Having lost the northern part of his own dominions by the hostilities of the Usbeck Tartars, he attempted the conquest of Hindostan with such success, that putting an end to the dynasty of

Lodi

Lodi at Delhi, he established an empire, which was raised to the greatest splendour and authority under Aurungzebe towards the end of the seventeenth century. The Mahrattas were a native Hindoo race little known till the middle of that century, when under a chief named Sevagee, they became successful rivals to the Moguls. The conflict between these two great powers was necessarily injurious to the English. Both the belligerents had fleets of galliots on the coast; these repeatedly skirmished in the very harbour of Bombay, and the factory was, in self-defence, occasionally driven into hostilities with each party. Surat suffered even more severely, the Mahrattas ravaging up to its very gates. In Bengal the English, thinking they had reason to be dissatisfied with the conduct of the native powers, resolved to seek redress by arms; but the attempt was unfortunate, and they were obliged to retire from Hooghley and take refuge at Chutanuttee, contiguous to Calcutta. After a succession of hostilities, in which the factories at Patna and Cossimbazar were taken and plundered, an accommodation was effected, and the English were allowed to return to Hooghley. Negociations for regaining their ancient privileges were commenced, but were interrupted by fresh hostilities. The contest between the Moguls and the Mahrattas had taken a decided turn in favour of the former; and Aurungzebe

Aurungzebe threatened to drive the English from his dominions. But the revenue derived from the trade was too valuable to be relinquished, and a fresh negociation for peace terminated favourably. Tegnapatam, on the coast of Coromandel, had been ceded to the English by the Rajah of Gingee, while besieged in his capital by Aurungzebe; and on the defeat of the Rajah the grant was confirmed by the Mogul chief: the English fortified the station, and it has since been known as Fort St. David.

The peace was followed by an event which deserves notice, as having laid the foundation of the future capital of British India. This was the transfer of the agency to Chutanuttee, to which place the British had retired when expelled from Hooghley. It was subsequently fortified, and in 1698 a grant was obtained from Prince Azim, one of the grandsons of Aurungzebe, of the three connected villages of Chutanuttee, Govindpore, and Calcutta, with the justiciary power over the inhabitants. These new possessions were forthwith fortified, and received the name of Fort William; and about the same time Bengal was elevated to the rank of a presidency. For some years the position and relative constitution of the British presidencies had fluctuated considerably; but Bombay at last completely superseded Surat: and from the building of Fort William the established Presidencies

sidencies were those of Madras, Bombay, and Bengal.

From its commencement the Company had been occasionally exposed to the competition of rivals. In the reign of James I. Sir Edward Mitchelbourne, for whose employment the Government had vainly interceded, obtained a license to engage in the Eastern trade, which was in evident violation of the charter of the Company; he however made but one voyage, and it appears rather for plunder than for traffic or discovery. By Charles I. Sir William Courten was invested with similar privileges, and formed an association which assumed the name of the Assayda Merchants: with this body, after some years of competition, the Company coalesced. In the reign of William III. another company was formed under a charter from the King, which was termed the English Company, the old one being designated the London Company. The rivalry of these two bodies was soon found to be productive of mischievous consequences, and the expediency of an union became apparent. This was ultimately effected, and in 1708 the two Companies were consolidated by Act of Parliament, under the name of the United Company of Merchants of England trading to the East-Indies. From this period the British interests in India may be considered as steadily advancing. The amount of trade and

shipping

shipping increased, and the intercourse and influence of the Company were extended. The warmest champion of Free Trade would find a difficulty in pointing out the disadvantages which resulted from the suppression of competition.

A period of quiet prosperity affords slender materials for history; and till the breaking out of the war between England and France, in 1745, nothing occurs worthy of notice. The first appearance of the French in India was nearly a hundred and fifty years before this period, when a company which had been formed in Brittanny sent out two ships; but the voyage was attended with so little success, that on their return the company was dissolved. At later periods the French made some further attempts to trade and establish factories: their chief rendezvous was at Surat; but the Dutch and English uniting against them, they were compelled to abandon it. They next attempted to seize on Trincomalee, but in this also they were unsuccessful. They were more fortunate in an attempt upon St. Thomé, a seaport contiguous to Madras, which they carried by assault. They retained it, however, only two years; but from the wreck of this establishment was formed their celebrated settlement of Pondicherry, where a small district was ceded to them by the native prince. In 1746 Madras was besieged by a French armament, and compelled to capitulate.

capitulate. Admiral Boscawen made an attempt to retaliate upon Pondicherry, which was unsuccessful; but the peace of Aix la Chapelle restored Madras to the English.

From this time the history of India rises in interest and importance. We have no longer to detail the advantages of commercial speculation, but to record the transfer of a magnificent empire into the hands of strangers, who a short time previously were supplicants for the privilege of defending themselves.

The territory of the Carnatic was one of the subordinate principalities immediately governed by Nabóbs, but subject to the Soubahdar of the Deccan, who was himself a feudatory under the Mogul Emperor. Nizam ul Mulk, Soubahdar of the Deccan, dying in 1748, the succession to the vacant province was disputed between his son Nazir and his grandson Murzafa; at the same time the Nabob of the Carnatic was opposed by a rival claimant. The pretender to the province and the pretender to the nabobship made common cause, and succeeded in attaching to their interests M. Dupleix, Governor of Pondicherry, a man of great talent, and of still greater ambition and capacity for intrigue. The combined forces of these allies were successful in a battle, in which the lawful Nabob of the Carnatic was killed and his eldest son taken prisoner. His second son, Mahomet Ali Khan, having escaped, implored and obtained the aid of the English. Such was the origin of the Carnatic war between the English and the French ; and it is remarkable that these two nations should have been engaged in hostile operations against each other in India, at a time when no war existed between them in Europe. As soon as intelligence of these extraordinary events reached the courts of the two countries, orders were sent out to put an end to the contest, and a treaty was entered into by which the two nations were to possess equal dominion, military force, and advantages of commerce on the east coast of the peninsula. The breaking out of the seven years' war in 1756 prevented the execution of this treaty, and the French and English became principals instead of auxiliaries. The French at first met with some partial success ; but the tide of fortune turned in favour of their rivals, who acquired, partly by conquest and partly by negociation, a considerable increase of dominion as well as of influence.

The English were at the same time obliged to have recourse to arms to defend their interests in another part of India. The Nabob of Bengal, Surajah Dowlah, attacked, and after a brief resistance, took Calcutta. The event has attained an infamous celebrity by the cruelty which accompanied it. The European inhabitants, one hundred

hundred and forty-six in number, were, in the most sultry season of the year, confined for twelve hours within a cube of eighteen feet, having no outlets except two small windows strongly barred. In this miserable den all, except twenty-three, perished. The city was in a short time retaken by Colonel Clive, afterwards Lord Clive, who had already exhibited proofs of that talent which raised him to eminence. Peace with the Nabob followed; but it was subsequently proved that he was in correspondence with the French. The English resolved to punish his faithlessness, by supporting the pretensions of a rival. This led to the famous battle of Plassy, by which Meer Jaffier obtained the nabobship, and his English allies considerable treasure and accession of territory.

Meer Jaffier, however, became unwilling to fulfil the conditions of his elevation, and he was in consequence deposed. His successor, who was raised by the same influence, was his son-in-law Meer Cossim, and it was stipulated that he should grant to the English, for the pay of their army, the districts of Burdwan, Midnapore, and Chittagong. Like his predecessor, however, he became hostile to the power which had raised him, and it was deemed expedient to restore Meer Jaffier. A war ensued with Cossim, in which the English were

were completely victorious, and Cossim escaped into the dominions of the Nabob of Oude.

The same year which witnessed the expulsion of Cossim was signalized by the conclusion of a peace between France and England. The former country was reinstated in the factories which she possessed in 1749; but the latter, in addition to her old settlements, retained the circar of Masulipatam and its dependent districts, acquired from the French, as well as the castle of Surat, the jaghire round Madras, the Calcutta zemindary, and the districts of Burdwan, Midnapore, and Chittagong.

The Nabob of Oude, Suja Dowlah, with whom Cossim had taken refuge, encouraged by some discontents which existed in the British army, decided on hostilities, and being joined by the Rajah of Benares, war commenced. The discipline of the British army having been restored, Suja Dowlah was twice defeated; first by Major Carnac, secondly by Major Munro, and was compelled to throw himself upon the generosity of the victors. Terms were made by which the entire territory of Oude, with the exception of certain districts reserved to the Mogul Emperor, was restored to him, and in return he conferred upon the British the dewannee of the three provinces of Bengal, Bahar, and Orissa. The

The word dewannee is derived from dewan, which was the appellation of the officers appointed by the Mogul government for the collection and disbursement of the provincial revenues, and for the administration of civil justice. These officers held their stations during pleasure, and were only stewards for the Emperor; but the grant to the Company was in perpetuity, and assigned to them the whole provincial revenue, subject only to the payment of certain specific sums. In addition to this, the Emperor granted to the English the maritime districts known by the name of the Northern Circars, though over them his authority was but nominal. They fell within the government of the Soubahdar of the Deccan; but having been the seat of hostilities between the English and French, the Soubahdar's authority was not well established. By negociation with him the Company obtained possession of this disputed territory, with the exception of a small part which became theirs in reversion. This cession, however, involved the British in new wars. It was a condition of their treaty with the Soubahdar that they should assist him with troops when he might stand in need of them; and in 1760 he applied for this assistance against Hyder Ali Khan, the sovereign of Mysore. The required aid was granted; but Hyder Ali, not less skilful as a diplomatist than as a warrior, succeeded

succeeded in detaching the Soubahdar from his English connexion, and prevailed upon him not only to conclude a separate peace, but even to enter into an alliance offensive and defensive, for the purpose of extinguishing the British power in the Deccan. Their combined operations were frustrated, and the Soubahdar deserting Hyder as he had done his former ally, made peace with the British, and retired to his own dominions. Hyder Ali then prosecuted the war alone, and entering the Carnatic committed dreadful ravages. Having diverted the British forces to a distance from Madras, he suddenly appeared before that place with 6,000 cavalry, having accomplished a march of 120 miles in three days. His further progress was arrested by negociation, and a treaty was concluded on the principle of a mutual restitution of conquests.

Our arms were next directed against the Mahrattas, who had invaded the Rohilla country. The British, acting as the allies of Suja Dowlah, drove them beyond the Ganges. For this service the Rohilla chiefs had agreed to pay Suja Dowlah forty lacs of rupees; but failing in the performance of their contract, the Rohilla country was added to the British conquests. A considerable tract of land was also conquered from the Jauts and other adventurers, by which the boundaries of the province of Oude were considerably advanced.

advanced. On the death of Suja Dowlah, which took place soon afterwards, the province of Benares was ceded to the Company.

A subsequent war with the Mahrattas was distinguished by some movements of uncommon brilliancy. A body of native troops, commanded by British officers, but whose number did not exceed seven thousand, traversed with success almost the entire Mahratta territory. Several fine provinces were subdued, and important fortresses taken; but war breaking out with Hyder Ali, peace was made with the Mahrattas, and all the acquisitions given up, except Salsette and the small islands situate within the gulf formed by Bombay, Salsette, and the continent. The war with Hyder Ali raged until his death, and was continued by his son Tippoo Saib; but the conclusion of a peace between the English and French depriving Tippoo of the hope of assistance from the latter power, hostilities were terminated by a treaty, which left the affairs of both the belligerents nearly in the same condition as before the commencement of the war.

The important changes which about this time were effected with regard to the authority of the Company would here demand attention, but as the due consideration of them would interrupt the narrative of the progress of British conquest in India, it will be sufficient thus briefly to advert

to

to them, and to reserve a more copious notice for the third chapter, which will be devoted to the constitution and authority of the Indian Government.

Tippoo Saib's restless character would not suffer him to remain at peace, and his invasion of the possessions of the Rajah of Travancore, who was under the protection of the English, involved that power in a fresh quarrel with this turbulent prince. The result to him was humiliating. After two years war he was compelled by Lord Cornwallis to purchase peace by the payment of a large sum of money, the sacrifice of half his dominions, and the delivery of two of his sons as hostages for the due performance of the conditions of the treaty.

The memorable campaign, which terminated in the discomfiture of Tippoo Saib, was succeeded by seven years of tranquillity. The enemies of British interests were not, however, inactive, but were employed in sowing the seeds of future wars. Among the most insidious and dangerous of these enemies may be reckoned the French, ever on the watch for an opportunity of diminishing the power of the English, and now intoxicated with the doctrines of liberty and equality which they had undertaken to disseminate throughout the earth. Even regions which for ages had patiently submitted to despotic power,

were

were not exempt from the intrusion of these opinions. The French ventured to establish a society in Mysore for the diffusion of the knowledge of the rights of man, and met with very different success to that which awaited the unfortunate Jean Bon St. André in the kindred region of Africa. They received from the sovereign patronage and protection. He even condescended to become an honorary member of the society, and was enrolled among its associates by the incongruous name of *Citizen Tippoo*. The result of these machinations was another war, which terminated with the storming of Seringapatam, the death of Tippoo, and the partition of his dominions. In the division the English retained the districts of Canara, including all the sea coast of the Mysore, the provinces immediately adjoining the possessions of the British on the coast of Malabar, and the Carnatic; the forts and posts of the passes into the Mysore, and the island and fortress of Seringapatam. Certain districts were given to the Nizam, which, however, were afterwards surrendered by that power to the English, together with other territories which had been acquired by a former treaty. A third portion was reserved to be given to the Peishwa upon certain conditions; but he having refused to accede, the reserved territory was divided between the British and the Nizam. The

Peishwa

Peishwa, however, was forced ultimately to claim the assistance of the British to deliver him from the state of anarchy by which he was surrounded. A treaty was in consequence concluded, by which the British consented to furnish the Peishwa with a certain number of troops, and he to assign a portion of territory for their payment.

The war which ensued for the protection of the Peishwa was distinguished by the brilliant services of Lord Lake and of another commander, who in the East commenced that illustrious career which he terminated by the liberation of Europe. The splendour of his Indian campaigns is indeed obscured by the surpassing glory that encircles the head of the conqueror of Napoleon; but no one who adverts to this period of the history of India, however briefly, can be excused if he pass by the name of Wellington without bestowing the tribute of admiration. Space will not permit a detailed recital of the achievements of the British army in these wars: it must suffice to record the results. In a comparatively short space of time a formidable confederation of French and Mahratta power was broken, and an immense accession of territory gained.

From this period the history of India presents little of importance until 1814, when the British became involved in a war with the Nepaulese, a people of predatory habits, inhabiting a mountain

country.

country. The nature of the country, the imperfect knowledge which the British possessed of it, the courage of the enemy, and the fortifications by which they were defended, were obstacles to the success of the British, and continued for some time to impede it. Military skill ultimately overcame these difficulties, and the Nepaulese being subdued, agreed to a treaty by which the British became possessed of certain districts deemed necessary to the security of their frontier; but endeavouring, in the true spirit of Indian policy, to evade ratification of the treaty, a renewal of hostilities became unavoidable. A war of very brief duration was sufficient to accomplish its object.

The constant wars and commotions prevailing among the native powers of India produced in great numbers men trained in habits of rapine and disorder. Gathering strength by degrees, these lawless ruffians became at length associated in bands under recognized leaders, and on the arrival of the Marquis of Hastings in India they mustered a force of not less than 40,000 cavalry. They were termed Pindarries, and in their predatory excursions committed the most shocking excesses. The irruptions of these bandits into the Company's territories compelled the Government to take up arms, and they were preparing to take vigorous measures for their expulsion, when

when the Peishwa, an ally and dependent of the British, revolted against their authority. The Rajah of Nagpore, who stood in the same relation to the British, pursued a similar course. Both these powers were subdued, while the war with the Pindarries was prosecuted with success. In the mean time the British Government became involved in disputes with Scindia and Holkar, two independent chiefs. With the former they made terms, but the treaty forced upon him was executed with extreme reluctance. Holkar resolved to have recourse to war. It ended in his entire defeat; his power was completely broken, and he was compelled to sue for peace. The army being now at liberty to act against the Pindarries, the dispersion of that lawless body was at length effected.

It now only remains to notice the war with the Burmese. This war, like most of those in which the English have been engaged, was occasioned by the aggression of the power with whom it was waged. During the Pindarrie war the Burmese were in communication with several of the belligerent native chiefs, and were even prepared for an invasion of the frontier of Bengal. This was averted by a stratagem. The Marquis of Hastings had received a rescript from the Burmese monarch, requiring the surrender of all provinces east of the Baugrutty. The projected hostility was evidently

a measure

a measure concerted with the Mahrattas. Lord Hastings sent back the envoy with an intimation that the answer should be conveyed through another channel. It declared that the Governor-general was too well acquainted with his Majesty's wisdom to be the dupe of the gross forgery attempted to be palmed upon him, and he therefore transmitted to the king the document fabricated in his august name, and trusted that he would submit to condign punishment the persons who had endeavoured to sow dissention between two powers, whose reciprocal interest it was to cultivate relations of amity. By this proceeding the necessity of noticing the insolent step of the Burmese monarch was evaded, and that sovereign on hearing of the defeat of his Mahratta allies was content to remain at peace.

But though the expression of hostile feeling was for awhile suppressed, the feeling itself was not removed, and the Burmese monarch now gained courage to attack where before he had been satisfied to threaten. War commenced, and the successes of the British led to the conclusion of an armistice which was employed in negociations. These negociations being unsuccessful, hostilities were resumed. The march of the English, as in Nepaul, was in some degree retarded by the nature of the country, but this obstacle being overcome, the Burmese sustained a complete defeat,

feat, and the British advanced towards the capital, when negociations were recommenced and a treaty concluded, by which the Burmese secured their existence as a nation, and the English obtained an extension of territory, valuable as affording a secure frontier. The treaty contained a stipulation for the payment of a sum of money by the Burmese, falling very far short of the expenses of the war, and of which a part only was paid.

The extent of British dominion and influence in India will be sketched in the next chapter. After all the declamation that has been expended upon the means by which they have been acquired, probably no conquests were ever made more righteously. Strangers were forced to become conquerors in self-defence. During a considerable part of the last century the question was, whether India should be subjugated by France or by England? To this question but one answer could be given. The perfidy of the native princes was another source of war and of British aggrandizement. But the crimes of these rulers have in this respect been beneficial to their subjects, by transferring them to the care of a better and a milder government. No friend to mankind can wish that the natives had remained under their old masters, and none but the most prejudiced can believe that their lot would have been improved by transferring them to the French.

CHAPTER II.

POLITICAL SKETCH.

A discussion of the merits of the various geographical divisions of India which have been adopted either in ancient or modern times would here be out of place, nor perhaps would much benefit be gained by following any of them. In a work, the professed object of which is not geographical, an enumeration of the principal districts is all that can be admitted, and the notice even of these must of necessity be brief and popular.

The most eastern part of the British dominions in India is Arracan, recently severed from the Burmese empire, which it adjoins. The contiguous district of Chittagong, with Midnapore and Burdwan, were among our earliest acquisitions in India, having come into our possession from the Nabob of Bengal in 1760. These were followed five years afterwards by the provinces of Bengal, forming in themselves a powerful kingdom, and giving the British an influence and authority which has gradually led to their supremacy in India. At the north-eastern extremity of this territory is Assam, which with Arracan was ceded by the Burmese at the termination of the war with that power.

power. A part only of this district is immediately subject to the British Government, Upper Assam having been lately assigned to a native prince. At the northern boundary of these provinces we arrive at the dominions of Bhotan and Nepaul. Goruckpoor, Benares, the Upper and Lower Dooab, Bareilly, and Kumaon (the latter newly-acquired from the Nepaulese), are the principal divisions of the British territory in this northern part of India. South of the Lower Dooab and the zemindarry of Benares, lie the districts ceded by the Rajah of Berar in 1826.

In the west, the British dominions extend from Ahmedabad to Cambay, and from thence along a line of coast extending, with little interruption, several hundred miles, through Konkan, Canara, and Malabar, to Cochin. The island of Bombay is upon this coast. More inland, Candeish, the Poonah territory, and the Southern Mahratta country, are incorporated with the British dominions. Coimbatoor and Salem connect Malabar on the west with the Carnatic on the east, which, with Tanjore, the jaghire of Madras, and nearly the whole of the coast of Coromandel, belong to the same mighty empire. The Northern Circars and Kuttack complete the line of maritime districts to Midnapore.

The influence of British authority is not confined to the dominions immediately subjected to it; it is exerted over nearly the whole of India by virtue of protective treaties with the native princes. In the states thus situated, the prince exercises the functions of sovereignty under the control of the British power, which is represented by a resident agent. The presumed advantages of this arrangement are mutual—the prince and his successors are guaranteed in the possession of their dominions; and, in return, he renounces all external connexions, except with the British, through whom alone negotiations are conducted, and by whose decision he is bound in all matters of dispute with other states. In some cases the prince consents to receive a subsidiary force; in others, this provision is dispensed with. But the great principles which pervade them all, are the supremacy of the British and the dependency of the native government. Subsidiary treaties exist with Holcar, the Nizam, the sovereigns of Oude, Nagpoor, Mysore, Travancore, Cochin, the Guicowar, and Cutch. The states under British protection, without subsidiary treaties, are too many to be enumerated. These two classes of protected states occupy a vast extent of territory.

It is to be lamented that the benefits that might have been anticipated from this indirect exercise of British authority have not been realised. Most of the protected states are wretchedly misgoverned, and there cannot be the slightest doubt that the people would be far happier as British subjects than they are now. The British provinces have been steadily advancing in prosperity; the progress of the protected states has been from bad to worse. In some cases, the reliance on British support encourages the sovereign to abandon himself to a course of personal gratification, regardless of the interests of his subjects. In all, the supremacy of a foreign power deprives him of that importance, which is necessary to command either the respect of his subjects or his own. Feeling that he is regarded as a cipher, he will not be unlikely to take the same view of his situation, and, divesting himself of all responsibility, to consider his elevated rank only as bestowing a title to unlimited indulgence—an exemption from every species of care, and a license to sink into irreclaimable apathy and sensuality.

The policy of the British Government in India has always been opposed to conquest. But though it is impossible not to respect their motives, it is equally impossible not to perceive that, had they been actuated by a less scrupulous spirit, the condition of a large portion of the people of India would have been far better than it is. Could the whole of the protected states be annexed at once to the British dominions, humanity would have cause to rejoice. Unfortunately this cannot take place without a violation of that good faith

faith which, in all parts of the world, it has been the pride of England to maintain. Occasionally, the accumulation of abuses in these protected states becomes so enormous, that the supreme power is compelled to carry its interference beyond mere remonstrance. It is not improbable that some change will be made in the relation at present existing between Oude and the protecting power. A long course of misgovernment having reduced that kingdom to a state of anarchy, the British may perhaps find it necessary to take the administration into their own hands.

It will be evident from this view, that the British authority in India is paramount. That of the French is almost annihilated. They still occupy Pondicherry, and one or two other places of small importance, but they no longer dispute with the English the dominion of the East. The Portuguese linger in a few spots, the scenes of their former commercial grandeur. The Danes have possession of a few settlements, neither extensive nor important. The Dutch retain Sumatra, Java, Borneo, and some other islands; but from none of these has Britain at this time any thing to fear. Her rivals have fallen before her, and left her in possession of the most gigantic dominion that ever was appended to a foreign state.

CHAPTER III.

THE GOVERNMENT OF INDIA.

THE East-India Company proceeded to Hindostan as merchants—circumstances converted them into sovereigns. On various occasions the ministers of the crown had shown a strong disposition to interfere with the government of India, and to participate in its wealth and patronage. The magnificent conquests which distinguished the middle of the last century furnished a fresh pretext for interference; and as men are never at a loss to find reasons to justify the course of action which they are inclined to pursue, the anomalous fact of a Commercial Company swaying the destinies of a mighty empire, was dwelt upon with all the energy which personal interest lends alike to truth or falsehood. Upon the intelligent and the unprejudiced such declamation would have little effect. No government ever existed that was conformed precisely to the principles of abstract reason: and if such a one should ever be framed, its endurance would, in all probability, only be sufficient to manifest the folly of the experiment. In all forms of government anomalies exist, and the question with regard to the

Company

Company is therefore only one of degree. Thoughtful men may in their closets frame schemes of government, which upon paper shall appear perfect, but pure science is only for the intellect—the ideal must yield something to the practical, when brought to bear upon the ordinary concerns of life. Instead, therefore, of expatiating upon the irregularity of merchants exercising sovereign power, it would have been well to inquire how it had been exercised, and how far the great purposes for which government exists had been answered. Some such inquiries indeed were instituted, but with little of that spirit of fairness by which they ought to have been characterized. It could not be denied, that the state of the people had been improved: but it had not been improved so rapidly as the opponents of the Company thought, or affected to think, that it ought. The work of a century could not be accomplished in a few years. Under the most favourable circumstances national improvement is slow, and the circumstances of Hindostan were any thing but favourable. Its native population had been for centuries subject to aliens, whose iron rule had raised an abundant crop of all those vices which are generated by oppression. They were the victims of one of the most odious and debasing superstitions that ever shed its withering influence over the human mind, a superstition which

which alike palsied the intellect and corrupted the heart: they were, moreover, both constitutionally and by principle, averse to change. Under such a combination of circumstances, it is more surprising that any advance had been made under the dominion of the Company, than that the work of ages had not been achieved in a few brief years. But such considerations as these, reasonable as they are, could not be expected to have much influence in modifying the views of faction and ambition. The golden prize of India was regarded by the Government at home with envy, and as early as 1767, some discussion took place as to the rights of sovereignty.

The year 1773 was marked by the first direct invasion of the power hitherto exercised by the Company. By an act passed in that year, the Directors were required to lay before his Majesty's ministers, from time to time, all correspondence from India relating to revenue and to civil and military affairs. A governor-general and council were named, and various changes were made in the constitution of the Company at home. Before this time, every holder of £500 stock was a member of the Court of Proprietors, and no amount gave a plurality of votes. The qualification was raised to £1000, and an increased number of votes given to the holders of stock to a larger amount. Modifications equally important were

were made in the Court of Directors. They had formerly been elected annually; they were now to serve for a period of four years.

The barrier once broken down, the flood of Parliamentary interference rolled on apace. The year 1781 produced a further change. In addition to the information required by the last act, the Directors were called upon to communicate to Ministers all despatches sent to India; and in all matters of war and peace, and all transactions with other powers, to be governed by their advice. This was an important step gained by the Ministry at the expense of the Company, and Lord North would not have been content even with this acquisition had he felt himself more secure in his ministerial seat; but he was then tottering, and not long afterwards fell. The ill-fated cabinets of the Marquis of Rockingham and the Earl of Shelburne were too shortlived to admit of any proceedings; but this temporary repose was followed by the severest blow ever aimed against the authority and privileges of the Company. Had it succeeded, it would have been alike fatal to India and to England; to the rights of the Company, and to the liberties of the people.

Forced by circumstances into power, the coalition ministry was disagreeable to the King, and unpopular with the nation. To enable them to overcome these obstacles to the maintenance of their

their station, the Ministers turned their eyes to India, a country which, at that time, afforded a field for the speculations of every political charlatan. A plan was accordingly devised, ostensibly for the better government of India, but substantially for upholding a falling ministry. By this monstrous scheme the Company were to be deprived of even the forms of authority. The two existing Courts of Proprietors and Directors were to be abolished. Seven commissioners, to be named in the act, were to be invested with the uncontrolled exercise of both the political and the commercial functions of the Company, the last being committed to the especial care of nine assistant commissioners, who were also to be named by the act. The chief commissioners, in whom was centred all the power and patronage, were to be irremovable, except by the King, upon the address of either House of Parliament. The assistant commissioners were to be removable by the concurrence of five of the superior.

The bill excited throughout the country a degree of alarm almost without precedent. It was regarded at once as a gross violation of chartered rights, and as an instrument for destroying the independence of Parliament.

The feeling of respect for corporate rights was stronger at that time than at present, and perhaps wisely so. Statesmen may sometimes find it convenient

convenient to treat them with contempt; but the experiment is always attended with danger. Every fresh violation of the rights of public bodies weakens the security of all private rights. The expediency which to-day calls for the sacrifice of a corporation, may to-morrow demand the sacrifice of an individual. Common safety is to be found only in common protection, and it is impossible to frame a distinction which shall have the effect of placing in security the rights of private persons, whilst those of public bodies are left at the mercy of expediency. The title of the East-India Company had originated in a royal grant. It had been strengthened by time, and by the repeated recognition of the Legislature; and the violent measure proposed by the Coalition Ministry could be justified only by the grossest delinquency. The partisans of the Ministry, indeed, treated chartered rights with a levity worthy of a later period; and the attorney-general ventured upon language which his own party felt to be rash, if not indecent. In one of the debates on the bill, the zeal of this functionary led him so far as to say, "What is a charter? a parchment with a piece of wax dangling from it."* Such language was not calculated to allay the

* A subsequent speaker, adverting to this, supposed a bill introduced to hang the attorney-general, when, said he, "it might be said, What is a hanged attorney-general? Nothing but a carcase dangling at the end of a rope."

the public alarm, and men would naturally begin to ask upon whom the next blow was to fall. Wherever it might be aimed, it was obvious that the passing of the obnoxious bill, by transferring the patronage of India into the hands of Ministers or their nominees, would enable them to strike with redoubled force and increased certainty. Mr. Mill has denied this assumption, and appears to think the degree of influence to which the House of Commons is subjected a matter of little importance. He asserts, that if the subservience of the House of Commons depends upon the degree, more or less, of influence to which it is exposed, it must be an ill-constituted assembly. It is so far ill constituted that it partakes of that infirmity which adheres to every thing human. But how is this to be avoided? If Mr. Mill believes that while human nature remains what it is, he can call into existence a legislative assembly from which all unworthy motives shall be infallibly excluded, he deceives himself, but he will certainly deceive no one else. He talks of securities; but the best security is the removal of temptation. The patronage of India in the hands of the Company is little likely to be abused; in the hands of the Minister for the time being, it would be attended with danger. Locked up for the benefit of a single political party, as proposed by the Coalition Ministry, it would enable that party

party to dictate both to the throne and to the people, and to fix themselves in power too firmly for any thing short of a political convulsion to displace them.

In this light was the subject viewed by the people of England, notwithstanding which the House of Commons passed the bill. The House of Lords, however, interposed, and rescued the crown and the country by rejecting a measure which would have enslaved both.

The fate of the Ministry being bound up with their India Bill, the rejection of the one passed sentence of deposition upon the other. The Coalition Ministry was succeeded by that of Mr. Pitt, and at an early period after his accession to power, the affairs of India were brought under the consideration of Parliament. The plan of the new Ministry was of a less violent character than that of their predecessors. The Company were to continue to exercise the functions of government under the inspection of the English cabinet, as they had done for eleven years previously; but, to ensure a greater degree of attention than could otherwise be bestowed, a Board was created for the express purpose of superintending and controlling Indian affairs.

The system established in 1784 is substantially that which now exists; the changes subsequently made being too unimportant to require notice.

The

The objects of the Company were originally purely commercial, and could they have pursued them in peace and security they would have sought nothing further. Their enemies compelled them to unite with the character of the merchant, that of the soldier and the civil governor. The British Legislature has effected a change scarcely less unexpected. In 1813, the trade with India was thrown open; twenty years afterwards the Company relinquished the field to their competitors. The history of the world affords nothing more extraordinary than the present posture of the Company. Formed exclusively for the prosecution of a desirable branch of commerce, it has renounced trade, yet continues to exist for purposes which its founders never contemplated. Called incidentally to the exercise of civil and military power, it continues to wield that power now that its original character has disappeared, and when it has no longer any interest in those commercial advantages which it was the single purpose of its conquests to secure. The act of 1833 suspended the mercantile career of the Company, and it now exists only as an instrument for governing the country, which the wisdom and spirit of its servants has annexed to the British crown. The whole of the Company's property, territorial and commercial, having been surrendered, its debts and liabilities are charged upon India, and a dividend

dividend of £10. 10*s*. on their capital stock secured; the dividend redeemable at the rate of £200 for every £100 stock, after April 1874, and at an earlier period on the demand of the Company, should they be deprived of the government of India. This last provision is of course a dead letter until after April 1854, when the present act will expire. For the better securing the redemption of the dividend, a fund is formed under the control of the Commissioners for the Reduction of the National Debt, termed the Security Fund of the India Company. For the purposes of this fund a sum of two millions has been invested in the public funds, there to accumulate to the amount of twelve millions. The Company are required to lay a financial statement annually before both Houses of Parliament.

Various provisions are contained in the act, especially relating to legislative and ecclesiastical arrangements, which will be noticed in subsequent chapters. It will be proper here to advert to the present constitution of the Company and the government of India, as settled by the last and preceding acts of Parliament.

The authority of the Company is exercised through the Court of Proprietors and the Court of Directors. To be qualified to vote in the former Court, a Proprietor must have been twelve months in possession of stock to the amount of at least £1,000;

£1,000; this sum entitles him to one vote, £3,000 to two votes, £6,000 to three votes, and £10,000 to four votes. The Proprietors have the privilege of electing the Directors; of making by-laws for the regulation of the Company, which are binding when not at variance with the law of the land, and of controlling all grants of money exceeding £600. The Directors are bound to convene a General Court on the requisition of nine qualified Proprietors, and such court, while it may discuss any matter connected with the affairs of India, has no power of rescinding a measure adopted by the Directors and approved by the Board. The votes are given by ballot, and in the election of Directors, a proprietor may vote by attorney.

The Court of Directors consists of twenty-four Proprietors, who are elected for four years: six go out annually by rotation, but they are re-eligible at the expiration of a year. The qualification for the office of Director is the possession of £2,000 stock. Formerly no person having been employed in any civil or military capacity in India could be chosen a Director until he had been resident in England for two years. The last act has removed this ground of disqualification: but if the Court of Directors, with the consent of the Board of Control, shall declare that the accounts of any civil or military officer are unsettled, or that a charge against him is under consideration, he is

disqualified

disqualified for two years after his return, unless in the mean time the accounts are settled or the charge determined. The presence of thirteen Directors is necessary to constitute a court, and they elect from their own body a chairman and deputy chairman annually. In the Court of Directors is vested the administration of the affairs of India, subject to the supervision of the Board of Commissioners.

The Board is constituted by commission under the Great Seal. The first-named commissioner is President. The President of the Council, the Lord Privy Seal, the First Lord of the Treasury, the Principal Secretaries of State, and the Chancellor of the Exchequer, are commissioners *ex-officio*. Two commissioners may form a Board, and the president having a casting vote, his power is consequently great.

To the Board the Directors are bound to transmit copies of all proceedings of their own court and that of the Proprietors, as well as of all letters and despatches received which contain material information, or which the Board may require. Copies of all despatches and official communications proposed to be sent out, must also be laid before the Commissioners, who within two months are to return them. If they disapprove or substantially vary any paper submitted to them, they are to state their reasons in writing. The Direc-

 tors

tors may then submit such remarks and explanations as they see fit, and the Commissioners are enjoined by the Act to consider them; after which they are to give further directions, which are to be final and conclusive. Despatches relating to subjects which in the opinion of the Board require secresy, may be framed by themselves and transmitted to a Secret Committee of three members of the Court of Directors, who are forthwith to forward them to their destination. In such cases, neither the Secret Committee nor the Court have any power of deliberation. But in other instances, if the Court of Directors shall consider the directions of the Board contrary to law, a case is to be framed for the opinion of the Court of King's Bench, which is to be conclusive.

Such is the state of the law. In practice, the intercourse between the Court and the Board varies somewhat from the prescribed routine. With a view to avoid unnecessary controversy, the custom has arisen of making what is called a previous communication from the Chairs to the President of the Board. This is an unofficial draft of a proposed despatch, which the President having examined, returns, either altered or unaltered, but unofficially, and without assigning reasons for alterations, if he has made any. The business then proceeds in the prescribed course. If the views of the Court and the Board coincide,

coincide, there is, of course, neither difficulty nor discussion. If they differ, the Board assigns its reasons; the Court either acquiesces, or states why it continues to dissent; and finally, the Board delivers its determination. Mr. Canning expressed a very favourable opinion of the practice of previous communication, as a means of preserving a good understanding between the two authorities to which Parliament has entrusted the government of India. He said, "The use and "object of previous communications is free dis-"cussion. They are amicable preludes to further "propositions, which enable the Board to state "its objections (when it has any), and to offer its "amendments and additions, without assuming "the air of dictation, and through which each "party becomes acquainted with the other's "sentiments, without being committed in point "of consistency and dignity to its own. The "official draft being thus prepared, with a free "knowledge how far it is likely to meet the con-"currence of the Board, the best chance is taken "for avoiding direct official collision."

Excepting such as pass through the Secret Committee, despatches generally originate with the Court; but the Board may require orders, instructions, and despatches to be prepared and submitted for its consideration; and if the Directors defer compliance beyond the space of four-

 teen

teen days, the Board may themselves prepare such documents, and the Directors are bound to transmit them.

The Act of 1833 was not passed without much previous investigation, and the ultimate determination of the Legislature to continue in the Directors the powers which they had hitherto exercised, may be regarded as an evidence that they had exercised them wisely. A body of men better qualified for the high duties which they are called upon to perform could not indeed be found. Many of the Directors have the advantage of local experience. They are elected by a constituency sufficiently popular, but at the same time perfectly inaccessible to those temptations which would not be without effect upon a class of voters less select. The number of Directors is sufficient to ensure a great variety of talent and information, whilst it is not so great as to impede the progress of business. But the claims of the Court need not be rested upon arguments of its probable fitness for the duties which it is called upon to fulfil: it may confidently appeal to history. Two or three humble factories extended into a mighty empire—a people steadily advancing to prosperity under its government—surrounding states imploring its protection, and seeking, under its fostering care, deliverance from the evils of native misgovernment—these are the facts to which the

authorities

authorities of the East-India Company may point as attesting their capacity for the high functions which they have been called upon to perform.

The testimony of Mr. Mill in favour of the Company may be regarded as unexceptionable. His laborious history manifests little desire to praise; but he is compelled to pay a tribute to the merits of the Court of Directors at home, and their servants abroad. To them he attributes all the good which has arisen from the British connection with India, while the evil he ascribes to that state influence to which the Directors have yielded—sometimes from an undue deference to the judgment of others, sometimes from the impossibility of successful resistance. The passage in which Mr. Mill delivers his judgment is too important to be passed over. He says,

"In regard to intention, I know no government, either in past or present times, that can be placed equally high with that of the East-India Company. I can hardly point out an occasion on which the schemes they have adopted, and even the particular measures they pursued, were not by themselves considered as conducive to the welfare of the people whom they governed. I know no government which has on all occasions shewn so much of a disposition to make sacrifices of its own interests to the interests of the people whom it governed, and which has, in fact, made

so

so many and such important sacrifices. If the East-India Company have been so little successful in ameliorating the practical operation of their government, it has been owing chiefly to the disadvantage of their situation, distant a voyage of several months from the scene of action, and to that imperfect knowledge which was common to them in common with all their countrymen. But they have never erred so much as when, distrusting their own knowledge, they have followed the directions of men whom they unhappily thought wiser than themselves, *viz.* practical statesmen and lawyers; and lastly, in the highly important point of the servants or subordinate agents of government, there is nothing in the world to be compared with the East-India Company, whose servants as a body have not only exhibited a portion of talent which puts to shame the ill-chosen instruments of other governments, but have, except in some remarkable instances, as that of the loan transactions with the Nabob of Arcot, exhibited a degree of virtue which, under the temptations to which they were exposed, is worthy of the highest applause."

In the face of such facts, it was seriously proposed, during the inquiries which took place previously to the passing of the last Act, to place the patronage of India in other hands. One suggestion was to transfer it to other corporations. It is is obvious that the only recommendation of this plan is that it would be a change. A more plausible scheme was to bestow the appointments upon certain schools and universities, and throw them open to public competition. Such a plan promised much, but would have effected nothing. Calculated to impress the mind favourably in the first instance, a moment's reflection will shew its hollowness. The degree of talent and industry displayed by boys, is an erroneous index to their future character as men. The fortunate competitors for school and university honours are not always,—perhaps it may be said not often,—eminent in after-life; whilst the men who have failed in attaining these distinctions, not unfrequently exhibit a degree of ability of which their early years afforded no indication. On a recent proposal to extend certain privileges to clergymen who had taken university honours, the highest authority in the church declared that a worse test of desert could not be devised. It is certainly as little applicable to the civil service of India as to the church at home; and had it been adopted, so far from ensuring a better set of men, the presumption is that it would have afforded a worse. If, indeed, the principle were good, it is not easy to conceive why it should not be applied to the patronage of the state as well as to that vested in the East-India Company. The former

is

is certainly not bestowed with greater purity, nor does it produce better public servants. The experiment is needless, and would end in disappointment; but if made, it surely ought not to be at the expense of a public body, who, according to the concurrent testimony of friends and enemies, have exercised their power in a manner the most exemplary.

The Directors possess the right of making all appointments of writers, cadets, and assistant-surgeons. The President of the Board of Commissioners participates in the distribution, not by law, but custom. The direct power of the home authorities is, however, limited to the original nomination. The advancement of the nominee in India depends upon the local authorities, among whom the patronage is distributed, according to regulations made by the Court and approved by the Board.

The late act prescribes a mode of filling up vacancies in the civil service remarkable for its complexity and uncertainty. For every expected vacancy four candidates are to be named, and one student admitted; and if the Directors do not within one month nominate the whole number required, the Board may supply the deficiency. The candidates must be not less than seventeen years of age, nor more than twenty. They are to be examined in certain branches of knowledge, and

and classed according to their proficiency; and the candidates to the appointed number, whose names stand highest in the list, are admitted to the Company's College at Haileybury. It would not be easy to frame a plan more efficacious in creating a large amount of disappointment, or less calculated to secure a competent measure of knowledge. For one who succeeds, three sustain the mortification of being rejected; a penalty which it is possible has not been incurred either by idleness or stupidity. It may be that all the candidates are sufficiently qualified, and three-fourths of them are exposed to the stigma of rejection, not because they are incompetent, but because a few of their competitors seem to be somewhat more competent; the supposed indications of such higher competence being extremely fallacious, and frequently the result only of superior quickness, not of superior knowledge. The hardship of this is evident. To those in whom the patronage is vested, the operation of the plan, though less personally annoying, is equally unjust. The candidates nominated by one may all be rejected, and those nominated by another all admitted; yet there may be but a shade of difference in their respective claims, or possibly none at all. Again, the plan does not ensure that which is its professed object, a reasonable proficiency in learning. The fortunate candidates

are

are selected, not because they come up to a certain standard, but because they are the best that offer. It may be that the acquirements of all are but moderate, and then the grosser deficiencies of some ensure the triumph of others one degree less ignorant than themselves. Happy is he who, possessing little ability and less application, has the good fortune of contending for admission in a year of universal mediocrity.

Admission to the College being gained, the student enters upon the usual course of study; and at the expiration of a prescribed period, such of the students as have a certificate of good conduct, are subjected to an examination in the College studies, and classed according to merit. After passing this examination the students are nominated to supply the vacancies in India, and have seniority according to their priority in the list, and, according to the same principles, have the right of electing to which presidency they will proceed. The Professors of the College are nominated by the Court, and approved by the Board.

It is somewhat extraordinary, that in these reforming times the College should have been spared, as its necessity is by no means apparent. The vacancies in the civil service are now comparatively few, and the number of students being proportioned to the vacancies, is, of course, greatly diminished.

diminished. Whether there ever existed any necessity for the College may admit of doubt: but it is quite clear that it is not adapted to the altered circumstances of the Company. It seems probable that in future the average number of students will not greatly exceed that of the professors and assistant professors, and to maintain such a magnificent establishment for so inadequate a purpose is only calculated to excite ridicule, or a graver though not more friendly feeling. The case would be different if the education proper to qualify the civil servants of the Company could not be obtained elsewhere; the public might then be disposed to look with indulgence upon an institution which, though disproportioned to its object, and exorbitant in its expenditure, was yet necessary to prevent the inconvenience that would arise from committing the affairs of India to the hands of ignorant men. But surely, in this country, there is no deficiency of the means of education. No description of knowledge is acquired in the College that might not be acquired elsewhere, and perhaps, on the whole, under more favourable circumstances. The only question therefore is, by what means shall the Company ensure a succession of civil servants, properly educated for the stations they are destined to fill. The most simple course will be the most efficient. Let the candidates be required to possess a certain

tain degree of knowledge in such branches of literature and science as may be deemed necessary, their proficiency to be of course ascertained by examination. But the examination should be confined to the positive acquirements of the students. Success should not be a matter of accident, nor should the same amount of information in one year obtain honour, and in another incur disappointment and degradation. The tests of proficiency should be well defined, and he who was prepared to pass them should have nothing to fear from the quackery of competition, where, though learning may sometimes vanquish ignorance, arrogance but too frequently bears the prize from modesty. Such a plan, though less showy, would be far more useful than that of the act of 1833. The required amount of learning would be secured, and none would be rejected but those who ought not to succeed. Seniority and choice of station are minor points of detail, which might very readily be arranged to the satisfaction of all.

Admission to the military service of the Company is not clogged with the difficulties which have been thought necessary in the civil service. The European officers of the Company's army commence their service as cadets, and they are eligible at sixteen years of age. Cadets for the artillery and engineers are educated at the Military Seminary at Addiscombe. They usually remain

main about two years, and on quitting the seminary are appointed to different branches of the service. If the demands of the engineer and artillery services fall short of the entire number of cadets, the remainder are draughted into the general service.

In the Committee of the House of Commons, 1832, some member threw out a suggestion that it might be desirable to make the whole service originally military. It is not easy to conceive on what grounds this opinion is maintained. The duties of a soldier and a civilian are very different. An individual is sometimes qualified to confer honour on either station; but his possession of the qualification for one does not necessarily imply his fitness for the other. Such a plan would be unreasonable, by requiring in the civil servant qualities and attainments altogether foreign to his duties. It would be injurious, by excluding from the civil service all persons, however well qualified, who did not happen to possess a taste for military life. In this country, civil office is sometimes held by military men, but their military character is accidental. We do not require those destined to diplomatic, financial, or judicial service, to prepare themselves by a series of campaigns, and why this should be advisable in India and not in England, no valid reason can be assigned.

It

It will now be proper to advert to the mode of administering the government in India.

The British dominions in that country were formerly divided into three presidencies: Fort William (Bengal), Fort St. George (Madras), and Bombay. By the late Act the presidency of Fort William is directed to be divided, and a portion of it to form the new presidency of Agra; but the division is not to affect the succession to commands and offices, nor the operation of the Mutiny Act.

The Governor-general is governor of the presidency of Fort William. He is appointed by the Court of Directors, subject to the pleasure of the Crown. His council, nominated by the Court, consists of four members, three of them servants of the Company of ten years' standing. The fourth member of council is not to be chosen from the servants of the Company; his appointment is dependent on the approbation of the Crown, and he is not entitled to sit or vote in council, except at meetings for making laws and regulations. The Court may also appoint the commander-in-chief of the Company's forces in India an extraordinary member of council. In the event of there being no commander-in-chief, or of that office being held by the Governor-general, the Court may appoint the commander-in-chief of the forces on the Bengal establishment. The Governor-

Governor-general in Council is supreme in India: but all laws and regulations disallowed by the Court of Directors under the control of the Board are to be forthwith repealed, and no law is to be made without their previous sanction, which shall give to any courts of justice, except those established by royal charter, the power of punishing his Majesty's European subjects with death, or which shall abolish any of the courts established by charter. The presence of the Governor-general and three ordinary members of council is necessary to give validity to any act of legislation. The other functions of government may be exercised by the Governor-general and one member. If the voices are equal, the Governor-general has a second vote; and in cases where he may consider the peace and safety of the country materially affected, he may, after certain forms, act on his own responsibility, in opposition to the opinion of the majority of the council.

The administration of the affairs of each of the four presidencies is committed to a governor and three councillors. The Governor-general is governor of Fort William, and has the power of appointing a deputy governor in case of necessity. The appointments to the subordinate presidencies are subject to the same regulations as that of the Governor-general and his Council. If the Court of Directors do not supply vacancies within two months'

months' notice of them, the Crown may appoint. The King may also remove any person holding office under the Company. The same power of removal is possessed by the Court, with the exception of officers appointed by the Crown. And the Court, under the control of the Board, have the further power of reducing the number of councillors in any of the presidencies, or of suspending the appointment of councils altogether.

One provision remains to be noticed; but as its probable consequences will be discussed elsewhere it will be sufficient to merely mention it. All natural-born British subjects are now permitted to reside without license in any part of the territories which were under the government of the Company on the 1st day of January 1800, in any part of the countries ceded by the Nabob of the Carnatic, of the province of Cuttack, and of the settlements of Singapore and Malacca. The only conditions required are, that the party shall proceed by sea, and shall on his arrival give notice of his name, place of destination, and objects of pursuit. A license is still necessary in the territories not specially excepted by the act. A British subject may hold lands in any place where he is authorized to reside.

CHAPTER IV.

AGRICULTURE.

THE restrictions on the residence of Europeans, which were necessary while our power in India was gathering stability, have now been abolished to as great an extent as prudence will permit, and British subjects are at liberty to transfer their capital and skill to a country where there is an almost inexhaustible field for the employment of both. England is saturated with the capital of which India stands in need. England abounds with the scientific information, and the practical ingenuity, in which India is remarkably deficient. England, too, possesses, in an eminent degree, that spirit of enterprize, the want of which is one of the most striking characteristics of the larger portion of the inhabitants of the East. For the employment of English capital, knowledge, skill, and enterprize, India presents a surface of vast extent and extraordinary fertility, with a supply of labour at once cheap and abundant, and it is to Englishmen that she must look for that impulse to improvement which, from her own sons she will never receive. The system of husbandry,

dry, if system it deserves to be called, has been handed down for ages unimproved, and, as may readily be imagined, is of the most wretched description. Where nature has done so much, man has done scarcely any thing. This has arisen from a variety of causes; the natural indolence of the natives; the darkness engendered by the gross superstitions which hold dominion over their minds, and the insecurity which at all times, previous to the reign of the British, has attached to the possession of property. In a country subjected to the three-fold curse of indolence, superstition, and anarchy, there is little temptation to accumulate capital, and still less to invest it in improvement. Dispirited by oppression, and enervated by fear, the native would be content to draw from the soil just as much as would satisfy the demands of his task-master, and afford himself a bare subsistence; while no stranger would risk his capital in a country where his improvements would enrich, not himself, but the temporary possessor of supreme power, or some of his rapacious myrmidons.

The wisdom and equity of British sway is removing one of these causes, and not only rendering property secure, but, what is equally important, convincing the holders of its security. This, however, is not sufficient. A people who have slept for centuries, are slow in waking to active exertion.

exertion. India possesses no class of men likely at present to take an interest in its improvement, and to effect this important object with speed and certainty the assistance of European capitalists is indispensable. The provisions of the late act regarding the settlement of Europeans may therefore be regarded as wise and beneficial. The restrictions previously imposed were necessary till we were strong enough to dispense with them. That period has arrived, and we have removed them in the spirit with which, on the return of strength or the attainment of manhood, we cast away the supports required by sickness or infancy.

The circumstances of India happily preserve it from the influx of one class of emigrants who find little difficulty in transporting themselves from Europe to the Western World; those who, bankrupt alike in fortune and reputation, seek a land where subsistence may be gained and character dispensed with. The distance, the expense of the voyage, and the absolute necessity of possessing some portion of either capital or credit, secure India from being visited by any great number of mere adventurers. Even to the laborious poor, India presents no temptation. The climate would incapacitate them for toil, and the cheapness of native labour renders competition impossible. The British settlers must conse-

 quently

quently be men of capital, and their immediate dependants; and the introduction of such a class of British subjects into the tract of country now opened to their enterprize, must be regarded, under existing circumstances, as promising unmixed advantage. The indirect benefits will not be inconsiderable. Every European must be a consumer, and thus give a stimulus to production. A body of British settlers will also tend to bind India more closely to Britain, by community of habits, language, and religion. Most of them will keep up some connection with the parent country, and many will entertain the hope of returning to it, while the increased intercourse that will take place between natives and Europeans must tend to remove the prejudices of both. We may safely then concur in the opinion of Sir Charles Metcalfe, that "every measure which is calculated to facilitate the settlement of our countrymen in India, and to remove the obstructions by which it is impeded, must conduce to the stability of our rule, and to the welfare of the people subject to our dominion."

The danger to be apprehended from the emigration of mere adventurers being small, the settlement of Europeans should rather be invited than discouraged; and with this view, it may be acceptable to point out some of the most desirable modes of employing capital. Agriculture is unques-

unquestionably the first; it is that in which capital is at once most required and most likely to produce a valuable return. But though India is rich in productions of almost universal demand, her resources remain undeveloped by the imperfect modes of cultivation, to which prejudice, ignorance, and poverty have condemned her. A volume would be insufficient for a complete exposition of the agricultural capabilities of India; but a few remarks directing attention to some of the more valuable and improvable of her productions, will not be misapplied.

Cotton.

Woollen was formerly the most important branch of manufacture carried on in Great Britain, and linen occupied the second place. In the vicissitudes which attend the progress of human industry, both linen and woollen have yielded to cotton, which now gives employment to a greater number of hands, and a larger amount of capital than any other commodity. To Britain an ample supply of the raw material is consequently an object of the highest importance. Equally important to the country which can supply the demand is the acquisition of such a customer.

The soil and climate of India are admirably adapted to the growth of cotton, and every variety is produced there. But from the carelessness and mismanagement which mark every stage, both of culture and preparation for the market, the price which India cotton bears is greatly inferior to that commanded by the cotton of America. Yet the cotton of the East is capable of producing fabrics of unequalled strength and durability. This circumstance may not be attributable entirely to the quality of the material, but in some degree also to the simplicity of the mode of manufacture. Thus the paper of Nepaul possesses the same quality of durability; but if manufactured by European mills, and bleached by European art, its superiority is gone. In the same way the circumstances under which the cotton goods of India are fabricated, doubtless have some effect in promoting durability. The thread is spun by hand—the weaving is performed by a hand-loom, and the process of bleaching is effected by steam and exposure to the sun. The injuries inflicted upon the fibre by the use of machinery in the first two operations, and of mineral acids in the third, are thus avoided; the cloth is not subjected to the process of singeing, and there is throughout no sacrifice of strength to either beauty or economy. Yet all these advantages would not confer the power of making a good article from a bad material. The low price of Indian cotton must, therefore, be accounted for on some other ground than

than that of its intrinsic inferiority—and the slovenly methods of culture and carriage are quite sufficient. The native will in all cases adopt that course which gives him the least trouble, and is attended with the smallest outlay; no prospect of increased profit is sufficient to tempt him to greater care, or a more liberal expenditure. In consequence of this apathy, the cotton of India is deteriorated in value—no care is taken to select the best varieties, nor the most favourable situations—no regard is paid to a due rotation of crops—a number of articles are grown upon the same ground and at the same time, to the injury of all—and the whole system of husbandry is of the most injudicious and perverse character. The cotton-shrub in India an annual, in America and the Leeward Islands is triennial. It is said that the best produce is yielded in the first year, and if it be so, the practice of suffering the plants to die annually may be defensible. But nothing can justify the neglect of changing the seed—a measure of indispensable necessity, but never regarded by the Indian cultivator. The methods of cleaning and separating the cotton from the seed, are as rude and insufficient as the mode of culture. The essential oil of the seed frequently escapes, and the cotton in consequence becomes dirty and discoloured. From this cause also it derives a tendency to become mouldy. It is further

further injured while in the course of transit. A large proportion of it is grown at a great distance from the place of export. It is conveyed partly by water in ill-constructed boats, insufficiently protected from the weather, and is sometimes warehoused for months at intermediate places. On its arrival, though some attempts may be made to clean it and remove the seed, they partake of the inefficiency which pervades every part of the proceedings, from the sowing of the seed to the shipment of the wool. Finally, it is subjected to powerful screws, injudiciously worked, and all the seed and other impurities with which it happens to be contaminated, are pressed into it. Shipped in such a state, it is rather surprising that it should bear so high a relative value, compared with the cotton of the West, than that it should fall so much below it. That great improvement may be effected by intelligence and care is obvious, but European attention and European capital are indispensable. By the application of these, there is reason to believe that the cotton of the East may be brought to rival that of the West, and one of the most important branches of our manufacturing industry thus be rendered independent of foreign states for a supply of its raw material. The weekly demand for cotton at Liverpool amounted in 1832 to fifteen thousand bales. The custom of the British manufacturer would be one of of the noblest presents that could be bestowed on India; whilst its transfer to that country would be alike beneficial to our own. The jealousy of our manufacturing superiority which prevails in North America is notorious, and it behoves us to guard in time against its consequences.

SILK.

On the production of silk the Company have bestowed great attention, and expended considerable sums. Private capital to some extent has also been applied to it, and with promise of success.

Silk-worms in India are fed not only on the mulberry, but also on the *palma christi*, or castor-oil plant, and several kinds of the laurel tribe. The mulberry is of course the most important, and the silk produced from it of a far superior quality. The culture of this valuable tree* is conducted by the natives of India in the careless manner which distinguishes all their agricultural operations. No care is taken to select the best species of plant—none to preserve it, or to obtain the largest quantity of leaf, while the worm often perishes from neglect. Yet land applied to the raising

* It is said that a dwarf-tree, the height of which seldom exceeds six or seven feet, is widely spread in China, and gives food to their superior worms.

raising of silk yields a higher rent than if cultivated for any other purpose; and though the reputation of India silk in the European market is not high, there is an anxiety for a fuller supply, which is enhanced by the increasing competition between the English and French manufacturers. Though perhaps in every point of view a less important article than cotton, it yet affords an opening for the investment of capital with a reasonable prospect of fair returns.

Indigo.

The beneficial effects of British capital upon India have been exemplified in the indigo plantations. The old Indian methods of producing this article were miserably imperfect, and it is to the connexion of Europeans with the Indian soil that we must ascribe the great extension of cultivation and the great improvements which have taken place in the mode of producing it. The effects of this connexion became rapidly perceptible. It increased the value of land, and raised the price of labour. The indigo trade does not, however, at present offer to the capitalist inducements equal to those held out by other articles of produce. Though the consumption of indigo in France has greatly increased, the supply is at present fully equal to the demand, and there is not much prospect of an extension of the trade. The price at which it is now afforded is barely remunerative, but its lowness has the effect of driving all competition out of the market. There are several plants producing indigo besides that from which it is now obtained, and should an increased demand arise, they will probably be brought into use.

Tobacco.

This article is an exotic in India, as is evident from the fact of there being no native name for it. Of its introduction, however, no memorial exists. The consumption in India is small, as the natives, though they smoke almost universally, never use tobacco but in combination with other ingredients. A very small portion of land is consequently devoted to its growth, as the quality is generally bad and unfit for exportation. That it might be greatly improved is the opinion of those best qualified to judge, and even at present India produces some good tobacco, though in small quantities. There is a kind grown to a very limited extent in the northern circars, and converted into snuff at Masulipatam, on the coast of Coromandel. This snuff is highly valued in England. Some good tobacco is also raised in Bundelcund. Capital, knowledge, and care, are probably all that are wanting to render the production of tobacco of marketable quality more general.

COFFEE.

The cultivation of coffee in India is of recent introduction, the first plantation having been established in 1823. Coffee being a shrubbery plant, requires considerable time to bring it fairly into the market; at present, therefore, to pronounce an opinion upon the subject would be premature. Bengal is regarded by Dr. Wallich as well adapted for its growth. The Hindoos at present do not drink it, though the Mahomedans do. There seems nothing improbable in the expectation that it may in time find consumers among the former class; and, at all events, the taste for it is so generally diffused throughout the world, that little difficulty in finding a market need be anticipated should an article of average quality be produced.

SUGAR.

The cultivation of sugar is already extensive, and there are few parts of India possessing the means of irrigation where it might not be successfully cultivated. The cane is quite equal to that of the West-Indies, but it is deteriorated by a wretched system of cultivation. The old mode of extracting the sugar is perfectly Indian—that is, of the rudest description. The West Indian process has been lately introduced, but no improvement will take place, either in the culture or the manufacture, that does not result from European

ropean enterprize and capital. To the employment of these no article offers fairer prospects. The consumption of sugar is enormous, and to its probable increase it is not possible to suggest limits. India may become the greatest sugar country in the world, and it is our duty to the people committed to our rule to secure to them this important branch of trade. The course prescribed by our own interest is not less clear. A large share of the profits of British capital employed in India, will return to increase the resources of our own country. The time, too, is peculiarly fitted for the experiment, and the present circumstances of our West India possessions urge it with a voice which it would be the extreme of folly to disregard. A change has taken place, the consequences of which are yet in the bosom of Time; but the best informed and the most sagacious regard them with gloomy forebodings. Some venture to predict that the period is approaching when all labour will cease in the West-Indies, excepting so much as is necessary to preserve existence, in a climate where the wants of man are few. It scarcely admits of doubt that there will be a reduction both in the breadth of cultivation and the amount of produce; and it is worth remembering that the great and sudden prosperity of the indigo trade in Bengal was caused by the destruction of the plantations

in

in St. Domingo. Previously to the French revolution, that island enjoyed an almost exclusive possession of this trade; but the disorganizing doctrines which convulsed the parent country extended to the colony. A revolt of the negroes was the result, and from that time St. Domingo has not produced a single pound of a commodity with which she previously supplied the whole world. Habit has rendered sugar one of the necessaries of human existence, and a prohibitory price alone can lead to a diminished consumption. Why, then, should we not avail ourselves of the advantages which India offers for the supply of an immense and increasing demand? Why, in the event of our West-India colonies becoming unproductive (a calamity which there is but too much reason to apprehend), should we not be prepared to draw from the fertile provinces of the East those supplies which are denied us in the West? It would be absurd to say, that the destruction of our West-India colonies would, in any case, be unattended with loss; but the loss would receive all the mitigation of which it is susceptible, by opening to the capitalist fresh channels of profit, and to the consumer new sources of supply. But to insure these beneficial effects we must be liberal—we must be just towards our Eastern possessions. Hitherto we have been neither. The duty levied on East-India sugar

sugar exceeds by more than thirty per cent. the duty imposed on sugar produced in any other part of the British dominions; the duty upon East-India rum is nearly double that paid by the produce of other settlements. The latter duty is, of course, prohibitory, and the former is a serious drawback upon the profit of the cultivator, as well as a serious impediment to production. These grievances ought not to continue. It is not just to tax heavily the industry of one half of our fellow-subjects, and to confer comparative immunity on their rivals. It is not politic to discourage a branch of production capable of affording extensive employment to capital and labour, and ministering to an appetite universally diffused. The admission of the sugar of India at the same rate of duty which is paid on that raised in other British dependencies, is called for by every motive to which a statesman should be accessible. It might be conceded without any apprehension of a diminution of the revenue. The increased importation would more than make up the difference between the higher and the lower duty. Such a measure would be at once useful and popular, inasmuch as it would not only substantially promote the benefit of India, but would convince its people of the disposition entertained by the government at home to encourage their productive powers. To the great body

body of consumers in this country it would be scarcely less acceptable and beneficial. If the period should ever arrive when the sources of our present supply shall fail, we shall be compelled to have recourse to the East. It will be prudent, then, to provide in time for this contingency, the occurrence of which must be regarded as something more than a bare possibility. If by excessive taxation we depress the spirit of production in India, all we can look for when the hour of necessity arrives, is an insufficient supply at an exorbitant price. If by an upright, wise, and generous policy we place her on a level with her competitors, and give free course to the development of her agricultural resources, we secure to ourselves, under all circumstances, an abundant supply of sugar at a reasonable rate. To the West-India colonists the question is of no importance whatever. If ruin should overtake them, it will not be in consequence of doing justice to India; it will arise, not from fair competition without, but from insubordination and commotion within; it will not be averted by undue protection, nor accelerated by a reasonable concession to another body of producers, whose claims are equally entitled to attention. The interests of India and of England demand an equalization of the duty, and not a single session of Parliament should be allowed to pass over without the performance of this act of justice.

TIMBER.

The forests of India might be rendered of far greater importance than they have hitherto been. Dr. Wallich, who visited many parts of India with an especial view to the forests, states that they contain every description of timber in the world, or a substitute for it. The wealth derivable from this source has been in a great degree overlooked, and even the timber most necessary for the supply of the wants of the natives has been neglected. There has been a serious falling off in the supply of bamboos, the universal building material for the poorer classes in India. With regard to other timber, almost all that was near the rivers has been cut down; but the natives being ignorant of the modes employed in Europe and America for the removal of timber grown at a distance from water-carriage, there is still a large supply inaccessible to them, but which would offer little difficulty to superior skill. Capital might also be judiciously applied in establishing saw-mills in the vicinity of forests, by which the risk incurred in floating timber entire down the rivers might be avoided.

On the other products of India it will be unnecessary to dwell. Wheat and barley are raised

 on

on a considerable breadth of land, but rice is the grain most extensively cultivated.

The attempts to introduce the cultivation of tea have not succeeded, and we know so little of the subject that it would be improper to offer an opinion. At present, the culture of this plant must be regarded as pure matter of experiment.

CHAPTER V.

MANUFACTURES.

The subject of Indian manufactures will demand a very brief notice. India is not calculated to become a great manufacturing country in the present condition of the world. Labour, indeed, is cheap, but however small the expense at which human life is maintained, the hands of man cannot compete with machinery in cheapness of production. The piece-goods of India, formerly an important article of export, are now superseded not only in the British market, but in her own; and Manchester and Glasgow furnish clothing to the people of India. The fabrics produced by machinery are not indeed equal in strength or durability to those manufactured by manual labour, but the vast difference in price ensures them a preference in every market. Some attempts have been made to establish cotton-mills in India, but the most sanguine must entertain great doubts of their success. The advantages possessed by the parent country are so overwhelming, that the contest is altogether unequal. Machinery may be constructed in England, but when disabled by accident, the difficulties of getting it repaired will be considerable. Time might overcome this; but there are other impediments not likely to be surmounted. The coal of India is of inferior quality, and with the disadvantages under which that country must labour in a career of manufacturing competition, she will do wisely to apply her energies principally to the improvement of her agriculture. She ought, however, to be allowed a fair chance of success. If we can do little to advance, we ought to do nothing to depress her manufacturing industry. Yet our statute-book contains provisions which have a direct tendency to this end. The injustice which excludes her sugar from consumption is extended to her cotton and silk piece-goods—the former are charged in this country with a duty of ten per cent., the latter with a still more oppressive impost of twenty per cent., while British goods are imported into India free of duty. If any indulgence were shewn, it surely ought to be to the weak. Here the case is reversed in favour of the strong. India should not be regarded in the light of a foreign country, but as an integral part of the British empire, separated by distance but united with it by a common interest. There should be no more distinction between Britain and India than between England and Scotland; and the subjects of both divisions of the empire should have the privilege of exerting their industry unrestrained by laws

intended

intended to favour one at the expense of the other. The duties on India piece-goods should therefore be repealed, and in doing this we should make no sacrifice. Our manufacturing greatness is too firmly established to dread any thing from such a measure. The actual advantage to India might be small, yet the boon would be valuable, as indicating a desire to give her industry a fair opening. As the produce of the existing duties must be inconsiderable, there can be no financial object in retaining them fit to be placed in comparison with the conciliation of our fellow subjects in the East.

CHAPTER VI.

FOREIGN TRADE.

COMMERCE and agriculture have a tendency to benefit each other. Whatever contributes to advance the commercial prosperity of India will stimulate its agriculture; whilst, on the other hand, as its circumstances are not the most favourable to manufacturing industry, it can only become a great commercial country by increased attention to the improvement of its soil. It cannot import unless it have something to export in exchange, and its powers of exportation must be limited by its power of production. With this view the improvement of agriculture ought to be a primary object with the friends of India. If this be duly encouraged, foreign commerce will follow as a matter of course.

The external trade of India compared with her capacity is not great. As connected especially with the interests of our own country, considerable importance must be attached to her commercial relations with China.

India exports to China vast quantities of opium, for the growth of which she possesses peculiar facilities.

cilities. Opium may be raised in Bengal cheaper and better than in any other part of the world; and China affords a market almost unlimited in extent. The taste for this drug has spread through the empire in spite of severe regulations for its exclusion, and is said to have extended even to the palace itself. However much this increased consumption of a pernicious stimulant may be regretted in a moral point of view, it is certain that it promotes several objects equally desirable both for India and England. This is not the place to discuss its importance as a source of revenue; but, commercially, its advantages are manifold. To India it affords employment for her land and labour. It gives also ready means of transmitting the tribute which she pays to England, and to that country consequent facilities for receiving it. The demand for tea in India is small; in England it is enormous. Here, as in many other instances, the convenience of the three countries is promoted, and their wealth increased by the agency of universal commerce. Bengal produces opium, and China desires to consume it; but in Bengal there is no taste for tea, which is the produce of China. In England this taste exists; but the Chinese have little desire for the commodities of that country. Again, India has to remit a certain amount of revenue to England; but the demand for Indian goods is limited: all difficulty,

difficulty, however, is removed by the intervention of that system of mercantile accommodation which has spread itself throughout the civilized world. The opium of Bengal is exported to China, where it is paid for probably in bullion. The holders of the bullion may not deal in the commodities of China, and the direct course, therefore, would be to remit it to India; but a bill is a more convenient remittance than bullion, and the latter consequently finds its way into the Company's treasury as the consideration for a bill upon India, and bullion thus deposited performs the office of paying for the tea required for the consumption of England. The importer of this article purchases of the Company in London bills upon China or bills upon India which are negociated in China, and with the proceeds of these which arise from the sale of opium, he procures his freight of that article which constitutes the morning and evening beverage of almost every class of the English people. The multifarious ramifications of commerce occasion many deviations from this course, and conceal the operation that is actually taking place. But whatever the details the principle is the same, and the opium of India is substantially exchanged for the tea of China. When the trade with that country was confined to the Company, the transaction was more simple, but in no other respect different.

Whether

Whether the British public under the new system will be better or worse supplied with an article which habit has made essential to their comfort, is a question which it is altogether foreign to the purposes of this work to discuss.

India, by exporting opium, assists in supplying England with tea. China, by consuming opium, facilitates the revenue operations between India and England. England, by consuming tea, contributes to increase the demand for the opium of India.

With England the trade of India has greatly extended, and in proportion to the development of her resources will it be increased. As has been already stated, the cotton piece-goods of England have materially interfered with those of native manufacture, and the probability is that the consumption of the former will continue to increase and that of the latter to decline. Both justice and policy, therefore, require that every encouragement should be given to the growth of cotton in India; and if she should be enabled to supply the vast demand of the parent country for the raw material, it will be some compensation for the loss of the home market to her manufacturers. Metals and woollens are articles of export from this country. The great obstacle to the extension of commercial intercourse between England and India is the difficulty of finding returns

suitable

suitable to the English market. But this difficulty is in a great degree created by faulty legislation, and would be removed by the adoption of a wiser policy. All duties that press injuriously upon the industry of India should be repealed, and especially so much of the tax upon sugar as places her in a worse condition than other countries subject to the British crown. The exports of India must be principally the products of her soil. In proportion as that receives the benefit to be derived from European capital, energy, and skill, will her amount of exchangeable commodities be increased. But the hope of progressive prosperity will be vain, if the parent country retard the course of improvement by ruinous imposts. It can never be too often repeated, that by advancing the prosperity of India we are advancing our own: by offering a market for the goods of India, we are opening one for those of Great Britain.

With France and the other European nations the commerce of India is inconsiderable. Wine is imported from the first-named country, but in many instances the consumers prefer receiving it from English houses of established character. The consumption is of course very limited, the natives not being accustomed to drink wine. The feeling against it is, however, wearing away, and some drink wine in considerable quantities. Any great

great accession of European settlers would, of course, increase the demand. The principal article imported by the French is indigo, and their consumption of it is on the increase.

The trade with America somewhat exceeds that with France. The Americans generally purchase their cargoes with bills or bullion—they take back indigo, silk, and saltpetre. Their demand for these articles is not likely to decline, nor is there much probability of their rivalling us in the commodities with which we supply the Indian market.

Some facilities have within the last few years been afforded to the trade with Ava through Arracan. The Burmese appear likely to be considerable consumers of British goods.

The commerce of India with central Asia is limited by various causes. The heavy duties levied by the various sovereigns, the insecurity of property, and the difficulty of transport, all contribute to cramp the operations of a trade which doubtless would extend itself, if aided by wiser government, greater security, and improved modes of communication. Caubul is a great and increasing consumer of Indian and British commodities. The manufactures of our own country have in a great degree superseded those of Russia, which formerly commanded an extensive sale in Caubul. Through the last-named country both Indian

Indian and British goods are transmitted to Bokhara, where the introduction of the latter has had the same effect, of displacing in a great degree the goods of Russia. If this trade were pushed as it might be, the supply of Bokhara with muslins and woollens might be secured exclusively to India and England. With a view to the extension of our commerce with these countries, Lieutenant Burnes suggests the propriety of imitating the Russians, by establishing fairs or bazaars on the frontier of our Indian empire adjoining Caubul, and the suggestion certainly deserves attention.

The trade with Persia might be greatly advanced. The chintzes of Masulipatam enjoy a preference in that country which ensures their sale, but there are commodities which Persia receives from other quarters which might advantageously be supplied by British India. Indigo and cotton are carried by the Dutch from Batavia, and the indigo is unquestionably inferior to that of India. The French, too, send various articles from their settlements. With reasonable care and activity, the whole of this trade might be transferred to our Indian possessions.

The commercial capabilities of our Eastern dependencies are at present very imperfectly understood, but a few years will probably develop them, to the joint advantage of India and England.

CHAPTER VII.

PUBLIC WORKS—MEANS OF FOREIGN AND INTERNAL COMMUNICATION.

WHAT has hitherto been done for the improvement of India has generally been effected by the government. The want of capital, and whilst subject to native rule, the sense of insecurity, have conspired with the tame and unenterprising disposition of the Hindoos to discourage all private speculation, of which the cost was great and the remuneration distant.

Much therefore remains to be done to render India what it might be, and as the probability of government being able to expend money upon public works is not great, it is to private enterprise that we must look to supply what is wanting.

The culture of a large portion of India depends upon irrigation. To promote this, tanks have been constructed in immense numbers, and the repairs and restoration of reservoirs forms a heavy charge upon the government. These tanks are constantly liable to accidents, and in one district of the Madras Presidency, North Arcot, no less than eleven hundred burst in one year, 1827. Such

accidents

accidents are often accelerated, and their disastrous consequences increased by the mismanagement of the natives. They are of course deficient in scientific skill, and practical experience seems in a very small degree to have supplied the deficiency of science. Independently of the heavy charge which these tanks entail upon government, injury frequently accrues to the cultivators from the delays which the necessary regulations of government interpose. Delay is ruinous, but it cannot be avoided with safety to the party at whose expense the reparation is to be effected. It is worthy of consideration, whether the construction and preservation of these important aids to cultivation might not be entrusted in many instances to private hands, with benefit alike to the government, the capitalist, and the cultivator. The ruling powers would of course take care that what was undertaken was performed. The present means of irrigation are probably sufficient for the land to which it is directed, but should more be brought into cultivation they must be extended. In this case a fitting opportunity would be afforded for ascertaining whether private or public superintendence could best accomplish this important object: a more important one to the prosperity of India it is not easy to imagine. The island of Ceylon has been greatly depopulated, in consequence of the ruin of the tanks. It formerly exported

exported grain—it now depends for its supplies upon the Continent.

Another mode in which capital might be invested, certainly with advantage to the people of India, and possibly to those embarking in the speculation, is the improvement of the means of internal communication. It is represented as being the opinion of the best-informed persons, that canals might be made in various parts with considerable benefit. One was projected between Saugor Island and Calcutta, and the line was carefully surveyed and levelled ; but from the difficulties which at the time necessarily discouraged the investment of capital in India, it was not undertaken. It has been said, also, that it would be neither difficult nor expensive to construct a canal from the Hooghley to the vicinity of the coal and iron countries of Burdwan and Beerbhoom, to which it would be extremely desirable to have better means of access than are afforded by the Dummooda, and other uncertain and dangerous rivers. Another plan which has been suggested is, for a communication between Calcutta and the Western Provinces by a line of canals. At present the communication is tedious and uncertain ; the navigation of the Hooghley is frequently interrupted, and the course by the more Eastern rivers is circuitous.

But canals must depend for their utility upon

a regular

a regular supply of water; and in many parts of India it might be difficult to secure it. In such circumstances, railways present an admirable substitute. Even where the difficulty of obtaining water was not great, railways might be preferable in cases where the probable amount of traffic was limited. The expense of such works would be far less than in England. In our country an enormous proportion of the expense, varying from a third to a half, arises from the purchases of land, fencings, parliamentary and law proceedings, and other causes independent of the mere construction of the railway. In India some of these charges might be avoided altogether, and others would be very much reduced. The actual expense of the work would also be less than that of similar undertakings in England. As the traffic would be comparatively small, a single road, with occasional passing places, would be sufficient; and as the weight of the carriages and lading would be much less, the rails might be proportionably lighter. Labour in India is vastly cheaper than in England; and, under these circumstances, the cost of railways would be extremely moderate. At present, perhaps, the use of animal power would be the most advantageous; but this, of course, would form one point of inquiry with those who might be disposed to undertake such works.

There are various lines upon which railways would

would be immediately profitable; and if the resources of India should be improved to the full amount of their capabilities, a necessity for fresh lines would be created, whilst the old ones would become increasingly lucrative. The extension of commerce demands additional means of communication, and the increase of means of communication facilitates the extension of commerce. The wealth and prosperity of India will be limited only by the amount of capital and enterprize applied to her improvement; and in no way can this be applied more beneficially than in connecting every part of the country by modes of communication cheap, ready, and certain.

Roads and bridges are works of less novelty, and they will doubtless be multiplied in proportion to the advancement of India in prosperity. Increased facilities of intercourse will tend to the improvement of the posts, and the substitution of better modes of conveyance than those now in use. Every where the state of the post may be regarded as a test of the state of the country. At once the result and the instrument of civilization, its improvement should occupy a prominent place in the views of every legislature. It is alike important, whether the attention be directed to its financial, its commercial, or its social effects. At present the natives make little use of the post; a circuma circumstance strikingly indicative of the condition of the country.

Connected with the subjects to which this chapter is devoted is that of steam navigation. It has been proposed to have recourse to steam, not only for navigating the rivers of India, but also for communicating with greater rapidity and certainty between that country and England. On each of these points a few observations are required.

The experiments which have been made on some of the rivers of India have been attended with partial success, but not sufficient to justify any very sanguine hope that the introduction of steam navigation will be attended with much advantage. The boats must be of peculiar construction to navigate these rivers at all. It is admitted that they must be confined to the carriage of packages of moderate size, and that all bulky goods must be excluded. From the impediments offered by rocks, rapids, shallows, and trees, they could not be navigated in the night, and the degree of speed would be very limited. Perhaps an exception might be afforded by the Indus. The ascent is not obstructed by rocks or rapids, and it affords means of communication with Central Asia that are invaluable. The coal in the vicinity is of inferior quality, but the supply of wood is abundant. There is consequently no physical obstacle

to

to the establishment of a considerable commerce upon this noble river. The moral impediments, however, which arise from the ignorance and barbarous policy of the states with which it communicates, are great, and these must be surmounted before it can be made the medium of diffusing the benefits of commerce and civilization.

The Ganges, the Jumna, and the Burhampooter present almost insurmountable obstacles to a regular and certain navigation. At particular seasons these rivers become torrents, and when the wind acts in the same direction with the stream, the united force becomes almost irresistible. With such difficulties, it may be doubted whether the attention and expenditure bestowed upon the attempt to improve the means of navigating these rivers is not misdirected; whether they would not be more beneficially employed in extending and improving the modes of conveyance by land. Roads and railways offer advantages which can never be obtained upon the rivers of India; and it is by these that the improvement of the country will be most expeditiously advanced.

The question of steam communication between Great Britain and India has given rise to much discussion, and on the practicability and value of establishing it, as well as upon the choice of the most eligible route, great difference of opinion exists. The three leading routes are, 1st, that by by the Persian Gulf and the Euphrates; 2dly, that by the Red Sea; 3dly, the usual passage by the Cape of Good Hope. From the first and last of these little is to be hoped. Round the Cape one steam trip has been made; but it occupied 113 days, and it does not appear likely that by any arrangements the time could be very considerably shortened. The expense, too, would be so heavy, that as a private speculation it would be utterly impossible that it could ever be made to pay: that it should be taken up by the government is as little probable as desirable— nothing but an urgent necessity for establishing such a system of communication, a necessity which certainly does not exist, could justify it. Steamers are much better adapted for short trips than for long ones, and the passage by the Cape may be rejected at once as ineligible. It has been well observed by Captain Wilson, that "no man who has had experience of long sea voyages by steam, or has observed the effect of long continued strain upon the vessels and engines, and also that of the protracted action of fire on the flues and boilers generally, would ever for a moment have believed it practicable that steamers could be constructed to make that voyage for a constancy with advantage."

The route by the Persian Gulf and the Euphrates has more plausible pretensions, but on investigation

investigation they are scarcely borne out. Bombay would in this route be the most convenient point of starting, and a steam vessel would proceed from thence to Bussorah, where another, of smaller size and of a different construction, would be substituted to ascend the river, either to Beles or Bir. From thence the course would be overland to some port of the Mediterranean; and Captain Chesney suggests four ports as stations, two of them, Scanderoon and Latichea, already available, and two others, Seleucia and the mouth of the Orontes, capable of being made so. Almost every part of this route, with all its variations, are open to very serious objections. Of the Euphrates scarcely any thing is known, except from the reports of Captain Chesney. The survey made by that officer is highly creditable to his talents and spirit of laborious research, but is scarcely calculated to lead any one else to the same conclusions with its author. It is evident, indeed, that the impediments to the successful navigation of the Euphrates are both numerous and great, and in practice we can scarcely hope to find them less than in prospect. Captain Chesney enumerates no less than forty obstructions, arising from rocks, shallows, and falls; and although this officer did not observe any fallen trees, such occasional impediments must be anticipated, as they occur in all rivers circumstanced

stanced as the Euphrates. Some of the natural obstructions are admitted by Captain Chesney to be formidable; some, indeed, would seem to be insurmountable, and most of them would occasion delay. Near Labtar Island the navigation is impeded by rocks, which render it necessary for boats to lighten a little in the low season. Near El Kaim is a much more important obstruction: a ledge of irregular rocks extends one hundred and fifty yards along the river, and crosses its bed with the exception of a narrow passage. The country boats are obliged here to discharge a part of their cargo, and the passage is regarded by the native boatmen as very difficult. A little lower is another ledge extending three or four hundred yards, broken and irregular, with a large rock rising above the water, between which and one of the banks is the passage for boats. Here Captain Chesney observes, "the steamers' paddles spreading above the water would have nothing to spare." A short distance beyond this obstruction is another, where the country boats usually discharge one-third of their lading. Below Tel Hafa Mountain, and extending towards El Wahadia Mills, is a bed of rock, stretching three-quarters of a mile in length, with a passage for boats of no great width, having a fall of a foot, over which craft are dragged with some difficulty. Still further, near El Madia, are other rocks, in passing

passing which it is necessary that boats should be lightened; and at the island of Karabla, a short distance from the town of Anna, commence the rocks and pass of Bahalet, consisting of an irregular shelf, extending along the river six hundred yards, the water being broken by several small falls, one of nearly two feet. The depth of water in the shallowest places is about twenty-two inches. The passage of boats at this spot is attended with great delay and difficulty. They discharge two-thirds of their cargo; and having effected a passage with as much as they are able to carry, return for the remainder, thus making two or three trips. Twenty or thirty men are employed to drag the boats up the falls against the stream; and Captain Chesney states, that "a "steamer must, in all probability, *be taken up in* "*the same way*, as it is doubtful *whether she could* "*work up with the paddles*." Seven or eight miles farther, the river is again obstructed by rocks; and boats discharge part of their cargo both ascending and descending. Below Hadisa, after a great number of minor obstructions, is the whirlpool of Elias. The water rushes over a rocky bottom, with a fall at the extremity of two feet in a distance of sixty or seventy, and terminates in a whirlpool directly in the passage. The descent here would, perhaps, be a matter of some difficulty, though it is said that the country boats effect

effect it in safety, merely making a half turn in the whirlpool as they pass. The ascent they never attempt, being dragged through a narrow and rocky passage by which they avoid it. Captain Chesney questions whether a steamer would be able, when the fall is at the greatest, to work up with her paddles, first passing the whirlpool, which might partly turn her round. If compelled to pursue the course of the country boats, her progress would be greatly impeded, the passage being very narrow and intricate. Five miles below the island of Jibba another rocky passage occurs, where boats are compelled to lighten. These are only a portion of the obstructions recorded by Captain Chesney. They apply, indeed, to the low period of the river; but it is impossible not to perceive that they offer very considerable resistance to a rapid and constant navigation. The Lemlun marshes present a difficulty of a different kind; here the river varies little in depth at any period of the year, as during the time it is swollen it spreads a shallow sheet of water over an immense tract of country. The difficulty is enhanced by the course of the stream, which is winding and circuitous, and full of sharp turns at short intervals. Further, the current of the Euphrates is rapid. During six weeks of the year a strong wind blows from the north-west, and this happens at the time when the current of the

the river is the strongest. Against their combined force, if a steamer could contend at all, its progress must be extremely slow. Captain Chesney thinks that he can construct a vessel capable of navigating the Euphrates at all times. This is doubted by other competent judges; but if practicable, the disadvantages attending the route will render it of little value. At certain seasons the passage must be tedious. Through the tortuous course of the channel in the Lemlun marshes, through the narrow and intricate passes between rocks, no one would attempt to steam in the night. Steam-navigation is expensive, and in return for the expense men expect a high degree of speed, and a tolerable measure of certainty. Neither of these could be attained on the Euphrates. The heat during three months of the year would be an objection to passengers. At Bagdad the thermometer is sometimes as high as 120° in the shade. This would be 130° on a steam-boat, a degree which few travellers would be disposed to encounter. But the number of passengers could not be great. Passengers must be attracted by superior accommodation. To afford such accommodation, boats must be large; to navigate the Euphrates, they must be small. Passengers would be further deterred by the necessity of a long and inconvenient journey by land. To obviate this, Captain Chesney suggests the

the clearing away the bar from the mouth of the Orontes, and afterwards forming a canal of sixty-three miles to connect that river with the Euphrates. These things might be done, but who is to bear the expense? This question will, it may be apprehended, tend to procrastinate their commencement to a very remote period.

The passage by the Euphrates may or may not be physically practicable, but however that may be, there is an impediment which mechanical skill certainly cannot remove, and in treating which it is to be feared political science will be alike at fault. The lawless state of the country would render the passage by the Euphrates, could it be effected, neither safe nor agreeable. The Arabs of the banks are more to be dreaded than the rocks and shallows of the river. The boats would be constantly exposed to plunder, and even if the passengers and crew were strong enough to protect themselves from robbery, they would be liable to constant and serious annoyance from the malice or levity of the lawless hordes by which they would be surrounded. This objection is felt by the advocates of the Euphrates line. It is freely admitted by Captain Chesney. He thinks, indeed, that the Arabs would not succeed in stopping a steamer, but he adds, with rather more coolness than seems suited to the occasion, "they might fire at her." The opinion of Captain Chesney,

Chesney, as to the probability of annoyance, is confirmed by the testimony of Mr. Hine, given before the Committee of the House of Commons last year. That gentleman, who resided in the country fifteen years, says, if the Arabs "saw "you were armed, they would not assault you— "they would not come down in any considerable "numbers, in order to stop you—for they would "know it would be useless, but they would fire "at you from the banks." And he adds the consoling assurance, that they are very expert marksmen. It has been proposed to compound with these marauders, by paying "black-mail." Mr. Colquhoun says, "the power of annoyance "with an Arab Sheik is an article of commerce; "he sells it, and often lives by it." The tribes, however, are numerous, and to compound with them all would be no small expense; and after the composition had been effected, the adherence of the chieftain could by no means be calculated upon as a matter of course. Mr. Colquhoun says, it "would depend upon whether he could "make more by breaking his promise." Mr. Bankes being asked, "could you trust the faith "of the Arabs after making an engagement?" answered, "I think as long as their interest goes "hand in hand with their engagement, I could; "but I am not sure that I could answer for them "much beyond that." The wild virtues of uncivilized lised life have been usually much exaggerated, and those best acquainted with the value of Arab faith, seem not to rate it very high. It may be urged, that a man's interest will in the long-run be best promoted by honesty; but this is not a view of the subject to be taken by an untutored mind. The principle of the Arab is (in the words of one of the witnesses before the Committee) "a "bird in the hand is worth two in the bush; if "an Arab gets one piastre to-day, he thinks it "better than the chance of thirty a year hence."

The land-passage is exposed to the same dangers in this respect as that by water. To elude them will be frequently impossible—to purchase the protection of the chiefs is a process, of which the expense is certain, while the benefits are doubtful*—to fight would certainly not be agreeable to that division of the travellers consisting of females and children, nor possibly to some who would feel more hesitation in avowing their dislike to it. This danger alone is therefore sufficient to render the route by the Euphrates ineligible. But it is due to Captain Chesney to say, that his various papers on the subject are not only creditable to his talents and industry, but exhibit a degree

* Captain Chesney says, that the Arab must be paid beforehand for whatever he undertakes, because he never confides in a promise, the natural consequence of not fulfilling his own.

degree of fairness which is still more honourable to him.

It remains to consider the route by the Red Sea, the only one which is in any degree likely to be made available. In this, as in the last route, the starting place would be Bombay, and with proper depôts for fuel, a steamer might work from thence to Suez without difficulty. It has been suggested that it might be expedient to form a steam-packet station somewhere in the vicinity of the ancient Pelusium, and thus enable the mail and passengers to cross the isthmus by the shortest route. This, however, is held to be impracticable, and consequently the only course is to proceed to Cairo and Alexandria. From the former to the latter place there are various routes; two by land, a third by the mouth of the Nile and the sea, and a fourth by the canal of Alexandria, which has been cleared out by the present ruler of Egypt. The land journies may be performed with tolerable expedition. The passage by the Nile and the sea is liable to some delays. There must be two classes of boats, one for the river and one for the sea. Another impediment is occasioned by the bar of Rosetta, which can only be passed in moderate weather, and with men well accustomed to the passage. The canal is navigable only during the high waters of the Nile.

The navigation of the sea of Suez being attended with

with some difficulty, Cosseir has been recommended as a port in place of Suez. But the harbour is not a good one, and its selection would render necessary either a long journey overland, or a circuitous route by the Nile. Suez may therefore be regarded as the best station.

The distance from Bombay to Suez being three thousand miles, cannot be performed in one stage. Captain Wilson proposes two methods of dividing it. By the first, the vessel would proceed from Bombay to Mocha and from Mocha to Suez. By the second, the distance would be divided into three stages:—Bombay to Maculla, Maculla to Juddah, and Juddah to Suez. This plan appears to be the preferable one. The vessel would be certain of carrying coal enough in the worst weather, and the strain on the machinery would be much less than on the former plan. By such arrangements the voyage from Bombay to Suez might probably occupy from twenty-five to thirty days, and from Bombay to Falmouth between fifty and sixty.

The plan is thus far practicable; but to what extent it is likely to be either beneficial to the public interests, or profitable to the undertakers, are questions which cannot be answered so satisfactorily. The necessity of this rapid communication is not very urgent, nor are the advantages to be derived from it very apparent; while the

outlay

outlay of capital must be considerable, and the returns, to say the least, extremely uncertain.

The carriage of letters would not alone cover the necessary expense, and the number of passengers cannot be expected to be very great. About one-half the passengers at present proceeding between Bombay and England are ladies and children; a large proportion of the remainder are persons in infirm health, and these would be excluded from the steam-boats by the passage overland and other circumstances. The intercourse between India and England is, indeed, likely to be increased; but many passengers will be disposed to seek the most economical mode of conveyance, which will certainly not be afforded by steamers. The passengers must also be sought almost exclusively at the place from which the vessel departs, as few persons will be disposed voluntarily to incur the fatigue and inconvenience of an unnecessary overland journey in India. Supposing a very rapid communication between England and India to be necessary, it would be indispensable that it should be constant. Neither by the Euphrates nor the Red Sea could this advantage be attained. For several months in the year we could not expect to navigate the former, and the latter would be unapproachable during the prevalence of the south-west monsoon. If it be not physically impossible for a steamer to make way against the monsoon,

monsoon, her progress must be very slow, and the wear and tear of the vessel and machinery ruinous. If effected at all, therefore, the voyage could not be performed with certainty, as to time, and the principal advantage proposed would consequently be lost. There is yet one most serious objection which applies to the two routes: they both traverse countries frequently visited by the plague. Upon the whole, there is nothing in the present prospects of steam navigation with India that is very encouraging, and it may be doubted whether the money expended in experiments by the various courses, might not be applied in a manner far better calculated to promote the permanent welfare of India.

There are some political considerations connected with this subject which imperatively press themselves upon the attention. The Russians are but fifteen days' march from the Euphrates, and although they do not require to be taught that the course of that river will bear them towards India, it may be doubted whether our appearance upon it might not give rise to jealousies which would endanger our peace, if not our dominion. In Egypt, perhaps, we have still more to apprehend. Some of those who have interested themselves in the success of steam navigation by this route, contemplate it only as a preliminary measure, and anticipate the completion of the

much

much-vaunted project for a canal, connecting the Mediterranean with the Red Sea. They seem to forget that this would strike a fatal blow at the commerce of England, or if this result occur to them, they disregard it. The discovery of the passage by the Cape destroyed the commerce of Italy and the Mediterranean. The restoration of the trade of the East to its old channel, would have the like effect upon those countries into whose hands it has passed. It may not be in our power to arrest the progress of events; but it is madness to accelerate that which is fraught with ruin to ourselves.

CHAPTER VIII.

SOCIETY AND MANNERS.

The Hindoo is strongly averse to change; the Mahometan, with perhaps somewhat less of constitutional repugnance to innovation, is wrapt in a bigotry which almost precludes his seeing any thing to admire in the habits and manners of an infidel. Yet, unpromising as are these circumstances, change will take place, even in Hindostan—in fact, it has already commenced. Imitation is one of the principles of human nature most early developed and most general in its operation; and though the progress of change in India will be slow—as, in fact, it is desirable that it should be—it will not be the less sure. In those parts of India where the influx of Europeans has been considerable, the natives have began, in some degree, to conform to the tastes and customs of Europe. Those who are able to indulge in the more expensive practices of the West, have manifested a strong inclination to do so. They wear watches; are fond of carriages and equipages; and, what is more remarkable, have become considerable consumers of wines and spirits. These

are

are matters trivial in themselves, but acquiring importance as indicating that a social revolution is approaching. We naturally imitate those whom we regard as our superiors; and the relation of ruler and subject is, perhaps, the only one which could have softened the prejudices of India against all modes of life alien to its own.

It is not merely in the minor details of manners that the natives are approximating to an European standard. They are anxious to form their minds upon European models, and to become acquainted with those sciences and branches of knowledge which enter into a course of liberal education. A strong desire has been manifested to become acquainted with the English language; a desire which certainly ought to be encouraged and gratified. It is proposed to make use of native agency in carrying on the functions of government, to an extent hitherto untried; and it is obvious, that to the natives selected for official station, an acquaintance with our language will be a desirable qualification. On many occasions, it will be positively useful in the discharge of their duties, and it will have the general good effect of producing a community of feeling between the supreme and the subordinate authority.

It may be asked, whether the intellectual advancement of the natives of India will not be inconsistent with the permanence of our dominion.

nion. To this question it might be sufficient to answer, that we have no power to obstruct the progress of knowledge. Where the desire of information is once excited, it is not possible to stifle it. It may be added, that it would be unjust to the people over whom we have acquired authority, to withhold from them the means of improving their minds. But, whatever may be the degree of danger attending the diffusion of knowledge, there is no better mode of counteracting it than by making, as far as we can, our own language the universal object of study. By doing this, we shall identify the people of India with ourselves. The great influence which the French obtained in Europe was mainly attributable to the wide diffusion of their language. It was the common dialect of Europe; and the universality of the French language paved the way for the universality of French dominion. The French language was every where spoken; French authors were every where read; and the best of them were regarded as exhibiting the finest models of taste and the highest excellencies of genius. The supremacy of French talent came to be universally admitted, and from this admission flowed a ready submission to French dictation. The extension of the English language in India will, in all probability, be attended with the like results. Its study will, of course, lead to an acquaintance with

with our literature, and our great authors will become to India what they are to us. The admiration felt for them will be transferred to the general account of their country, which will thus become associated in the mind of the educated Hindoo with all that is high in intellect and pure in feeling. This will be a far better guarantee for the security of our dominion than ignorance can offer.

A taste for our literature has already begun to diffuse itself. It appears that no inconsiderable portion of the young men of the more respectable classes speak our language fluently, and are familiar with our best authors, including those who might be supposed to be least adapted to Oriental taste, Dryden and Pope, and those more especially national, Shakespeare and Milton. To encourage and extend this taste will be true policy. The mind of England has impressed itself indelibly upon the broad plains of America. It may yet awaken the slumbering energies of India; and the names of our poets and philosophers, which are now resounded on the shores of the Mississippi and St. Lawrence, may be re-echoed from the Ganges and Burhampooter.

Connected with the diffusion of a taste for reading and for the study of the English language, is the subject of the periodical press. Whether or not it should be entirely free from restraint, is a question

question on which difference of opinion may be expected to exist, and with regard to which, those who differ should exercise mutual candour and forbearance. In this country, and in the age in which we live, the current of opinion, of course, runs in favour of unlimited freedom; and those who think that any restraint should be imposed, will admit that it should be to no greater extent than is absolutely essential to the safety of the state. There are circumstances connected with the state of society in India, that place it beyond the reach of those arguments, which prove the expediency of a perfectly unfettered press here. Yet it is not uncommon to find the question argued as though the circumstances of the two countries were precisely similar. If India be entitled to a free press because the press in England is free, by the same rule, she is entitled to a representative government, because England possesses one. Few persons will contend that she is at present fitted for such a government, though she may, at some future period, become so. No country should be deprived of the advantages of free institutions, but in proportion as it is unfit for them; and no greater degree of restraint should be imposed upon either a nation or an individual than is necessary to secure the ends for which government exists. To inflict what is unnecessary is tyranny; to concede what is mischievous is weakness.

ness. Freedom of discussion is a plausible phrase; but it should be recollected, that what is contended for is sometimes not freedom of discussion but freedom of abuse. The experiment, however, is now in progress, and it is to be hoped that it may be justified by success.

From the relation in which we stand to India our moral power is great; but we must not overrate it, nor by straining it too far, run the hazard of losing it altogether. There is much in Indian society which it would be desirable to change—much that, according to the modes of thinking prevalent in modern Europe, is unfit to be permitted. But we must not expect to alter the face of society by a word; we must not expect to accomplish at once that which must be the gradual result of time and circumstances; we must be patient as well as persevering, and not, in our zeal to eradicate abuses, incur evils worse than those to which we refuse a temporary toleration. Slavery is unquestionably an evil; but in India it exists in its mildest form, and its extent is not great. The humanity of the Legislature has directed that measures shall be taken for its mitigation and ultimate extinction; but prudence has forbidden any premature and violent steps, which might endanger the peace and well-being of the community, without promoting the benefit of any part of it. The end is good; and it is desirable that

that the means should be wise. Slavery in Europe has disappeared before the light of Christian civilization, and wherever that light extends the same effect will follow.

The friends of India have the gratification of knowing that she is advancing in knowledge and in freedom: they have but one further wish, that her moral improvement may correspond with her intellectual and civil advancement. This must be the result of higher principles than human wisdom can supply, and the means of promoting it will be discussed in the ensuing chapter.

CHAPTER IX.

RELIGION AND MORALS.

THE moral and religious picture of India is a dark one. The character of the natives has sometimes indeed been pourtrayed in an amiable and attractive light; but such representations have proceeded from persons either ignorant of the facts, or having a purpose to serve by mis-stating them. Nearly all well-informed and unprejudiced reporters agree in representing the moral state of India as most lamentable; and the few who deliver a more favourable opinion when speaking generally, on descending to particulars, admit all the facts which justify the harsher conclusion. It must not be supposed that those who speak with the greatest severity of the prevalent vices of Indian society, wish to exaggerate them, or feel any pleasure in the view which they are compelled to take. But there is neither justice nor policy—there is neither true charity nor genuine liberality in casting a cloak over that which ought to be exposed, in order that it may be amended. If we would effect a cure, we must not deny the virulence of the disease. It may be painful

painful to those of kindly feelings to think harshly of their fellow-men; it may be annoying to the hunters after popular applause, to subject themselves to the charge of illiberality; but the lover of truth will pursue his object wherever it may lead him, and deliver unhesitatingly the result of his enquiries, though it may not be such as will be gratifying either to himself or to others.

There is no virtue in which the natives are more universally deficient than in a regard for truth. Veracity is, in fact, almost unknown. Falsehood pervades all the intercourse of private life, and is carried to such an extent in courts of law, as to render it almost impossible for the judges to exercise their duty in such a manner as to satisfy their consciences. False testimony is not the exception, but the rule; and it is delivered, and even persevered in, with a calmness, a self-possession, and an air of sincerity which would disarm suspicion, were it not that two conflicting stories cannot both be true, and that the character of Indian witnesses is tolerably appreciated by those most accustomed to them. Not only will two sets of witnesses give directly contrary testimony, but not unfrequently will it turn out, upon investigation, that neither of them know any thing of the matter in question. Even those who have a just cause, will seek to defend it by falsehood. It must be quite unnecessary to descant upon

upon the low state of moral principle that must be prevalent where such things are of frequent occurrence. No virtue is more essential to the well-being of society than a general regard to truth. When this is wanting, all rights are insecure, and courts of law may be made the instruments of the grossest injustice. The tenure of property is nearly as uncertain as it would be in the absence of all law; the only difference being, that in the one case it is taken by force, in the other it is transferred by fraud.

From the prevalence of falsehood in legal proceedings, it will be inferred, that honesty is not in higher estimation than truth; and according to the most accurate and intelligent observers, trick, deception, and fraud, are interwoven with almost all transactions of business. In every bargain, fraud is apprehended; and it is to be feared that there are few in which it is not contemplated. The consequence is, that conditions and securities are multiplied without end, and the ingenuity displayed in devising precautions against fraud is only exceeded by the ingenuity exercised in evading them. If confidence is reposed, it is but too often accepted only for the purpose of abusing it. The agent or steward of a rich man endeavours to transfer as much as possible of his master's wealth to his own coffers. He again is plundered by his subordinates; and this

this is the course of procedure down to the lowest dependent, who having none beneath him, enjoys the luxury of plundering without being plundered in return. The dearest ties of consanguinity afford no security. The brother cannot safely trust the brother, the uncle the nephew, nor even the father the son. Trusts of the most solemn character are commonly abused; and the offices of guardian and executor converted into sources of emolument without hesitation and without shame.

Breaches of moral obligation are indeed too frequent every where: but nothing can mark more strongly the difference between Europe and India in this respect than the state of public opinion. In Europe, though falsehood and fraud exist, the imputation of either is disgraceful. The habitual liar will defend his veracity with warmth, and feels, or affects to feel, the charge of falsehood as an insult. The swindler would, if possible, pass for an honest man, and all who violate the laws of sound morality, pay to them an indirect homage, by endeavouring to assume the virtues which they have not. In India this is not the case. There is little more of decency than of morality. Men do not even pretend to truth and honesty, because the pretension is not necessary to their station in society. The virtues themselves are not respected, and therefore no one is respected

respected for possessing them, nor despised for wanting them. The wholesome check derived from public opinion can be wanting only in a very depraved state of society, and, when once destroyed, it is obvious that the scale of morality will continue to descend with fearful rapidity. In Europe, bad men are sometimes withheld solely by this check from actions injurious to society. In the better disposed it is an important auxiliary to good conduct; and with that numerous class who hover between virtue and vice, not insensible to the claims of the one, and at the same time little able to resist the temptations of the other, it throws the preponderating weight on the right side. The influence of habit, moreover, is not to be despised, and those who first adhere to truth and justice, only because it is decent, may in time become attached to the same course, because it is right. Too many, indeed, form their standard of morals exclusively from the customs of their country, and where the most important moral qualities find no echo in public sentiment, it requires little sagacity to pronounce an accurate judgment on the state of society.

While abundantly productive of the meaner vices, the Indian character is not exempt from those of a darker hue. Falsehood and dishonesty are associated with malevolence; and contention, animosity, and revenge prevail among every grade

and

and condition. Men pursue each other with the most deadly enmity, and with the most determined and long-continued perseverance. No opinion was ever more unfounded than that which has been so often advanced, and so commonly received, of the mild and benevolent character of the Hindoos. Passive, indeed, they are, and frequently servile, but not mild. Where they have any thing to hope or any thing to fear, where the expression of resentment would expose them to danger or inconvenience, they can conceal it, and submit to insult and injury with an appearance of the most patient submission; but the desire of revenge, though hidden, is active, and at the first favourable opportunity will be indulged. Nothing would be more easy than to produce numerous instances of the obstinate malignity which marks the Hindoo character, and which is confirmed and fortified by superstition. With all the delicacy which the British Government has at all times observed towards the religion of the majority, it has been found impossible to avoid occasionally interfering to suppress practices originating in vindictive feeling, and sanctioned by superstitious credulity, which threatened completely to paralyse the operation of the law. One of these was common in the province of Benares, where the Brahmins were held in the highest reverence, and their persons regarded as inviolable.

inviolable. When any process from the judicial or fiscal authorities was to be executed upon a Brahmin, he would threaten to inflict personal violence, sometimes extending to suicide on himself if the officer approached too near; or if, as frequently happened, his affection for his own person was too tender to allow him to place it in jeopardy, he would bring forward some member of his family or tribe whom he threatened to maim or put to death, if an attempt were made to serve the process. These threats were not mere words; they were often carried into execution, the victims themselves acquiescing, under a conviction, that after death they should become the tormentors of those who were the occasion of their being sacrificed. A practice, somewhat similar, was that of a person placing himself at the door of another, armed with some offensive weapon, or provided with poison, for the purpose either of recovering a debt or extorting a donation. By the established rules, the besieger was to remain fasting until his object was obtained, and the person besieged was also to abstain from nourishment until the other party was satisfied. During the siege, ingress to the house and egress from it were suspended. Neither could be attempted, except at the risk of the party, without wounding himself with the weapon, or swallowing the poison which he had provided. These two customs were found

so

so dangerous as to call for the interposition of the supreme authority to put them down.

Some instances, not very dissimilar, which before the Committee of the House of Commons in 1832 were mentioned with approbation, seem rather to merit the expression of a contrary sentiment. One of the chiefs of Telinga, on no greater provocation than an attempt to disarm him when entering a court of justice, plunged his weapon into his heart, and fell dead in the presence of the judge on the bench. On another occasion, when a military force endeavoured to carry into execution a judicial process in the Nellore district, a chieftain destroyed all his family as well as himself. The gentleman by whom these instances were quoted, regarded them as indicating the possession of a nice sense of honour. They rather indicate an overweening pride, and a fierce, bitter, and malignant spirit; and as these instances occurred among those whom the witness represented as the best and most estimable of the inhabitants of India, we may conceive that in those provinces where the native character is inferior, deeds of even greater ferocity are not unknown. That spirit of litigiousness which all admit to prevail in India more generally than in any other country in the world, is but a petty manifestation of that mixture of pride and malignity which, on other occasions, by a more elevated display, has succeeded

ceeded in confounding the moral sentiments of the European observer, and concealed beneath the barbarous grandeur of the act, the base and hateful character of the motive. Of all people the Hindoos are the most prone to litigation. A large number of the suits originate in malevolence or in fraud, and whatever their origin, the interests of both parties are almost invariably upheld by such a degree of mendacity as in the most corrupt parts of Europe is scarcely conceivable. Under these circumstances, it is almost impossible to keep the course of justice tolerably pure. The highest sagacity in the judges, combined with the most rigid impartiality and the most scrupulous care, can scarcely preserve courts of justice from degenerating into something very different from the name they bear. What they must have been before the establishment of the British authority, when justice was notoriously and almost avowedly bought and sold, is sufficiently clear.

It is a lamentable truth, that the feelings of the Hindoo are exclusively for himself. Sensibility for others he has none. His humanity to the inferior animals has been greatly extolled by those whose observation has been partial, or who have possessed no means of observation at all. This, like many other virtues ascribed to the Hindoo character, is not merely exaggerated, but altogether unfounded in fact. Certain animals,

mals, which his unholy superstition has rendered sacred, receive from the Hindoo as much attention and respect as he would award to the highest caste of his own species. But, with these exceptions, the brute creation in India are treated with the greatest cruelty. Even the beast which an execrable religion elevates to divine honours is not exempted from the general lot. The labouring oxen are subjected to treatment which in this country would call forth the indignation and horror of the lowest and most unfeeling classes. The Hindoo has no sentiment. He acknowledges and knows nothing beyond positive obligation. He is commanded to reverence a beast, and he obeys. He is not commanded to treat with humanity the same beast labouring for his benefit, and no feeling exists to supply the deficiency of positive precept.

To his own species the Hindoo is almost invariably cold and unfeeling. Estranged from his fellow-man by the exclusive spirit of a frightful superstition, he regards human suffering with a callous insensibility which is truly horrible. Some examples related by Bishop Heber are absolutely appalling. Such instances as the following, throw more light upon the real character of the people, than all the eloquence that has been expended upon the kindness and benevolence of the Hindoos. "A traveller falls down sick in the

the streets of a village (I am mentioning a fact which happened ten days ago); nobody knows what caste he is of, therefore nobody goes near him, lest they should become polluted; he wastes to death before the eyes of a whole community, unless the jackals take courage from his helpless state to finish him a little sooner; and perhaps, as happened in the case to which I allude, the children are allowed to pelt him with stones and mud. The man of whom I am speaking was found in this state, and taken care of by a passing European; but if he had died, his skeleton would have lain in the streets till the vultures carried it away, or the magistrates ordered it to be thrown into the river."

A second anecdote rests on the same authority. "A friend of mine, some months ago, found a miserable wretch, a groom out of employ, who had crept, sick of a dysentery, into his court-yard. He had there remained in a corner, on the pavement, two days and nights. Perhaps twenty servants had been eating their meals daily within six yards of him, yet none had relieved him, none had so much as carried him into the shelter of one of the out-houses, nor had any taken the trouble to tell their master. When reproved for this, the answer was, "He was not our kinsman." "Whose business was it?" "How did we know that Sahib would like to to be troubled?" What must be the state of moral feeling where such things occur? That they do occur is unquestionable. The high character of Bishop Heber, and his truly kind and amiable disposition, exempt his narrative from the slightest suspicion of exaggeration; he evidently relates the facts reluctantly, and would, if possible, soften their hideous character. He says, "I only mention these instances, because none of those who heard them seemed to think them unusual or extraordinary; because in a Christian country I think they could not have happened; and because they naturally arise from the genius of the national religion, which, by the distinction it establishes, makes men worse than indifferent to each other."

With the knowledge of other facts, which unhappily are too well authenticated, we need not, indeed, feel surprise at these. Those who are destitute of affection for their own offspring, can scarcely be expected to evince much sensibility for strangers; and though exceptions undoubtedly occur, one general characteristic of the Hindoo is a deficiency of natural affection. Almost every where but in India parental affection is one of the most powerful impulses of human nature—sometimes so powerful as to overcome even the attachment to life itself. The differences of climate, of colour, of civilization, and of creed, seem, in general,

general, to have little effect in modifying this passion; and whether in the regions of eternal snow, or beneath the burning rays of a tropical sun; among the fair-haired children of the North, or the sable and woolly natives of Africa; in the polished scenes of elegance and refinement, or in the hut where human nature exists in a condition scarcely superior to that of the beasts of the field; under the light of revealed truth, or in the darkness of ignorance and superstition; in every possible variety of situation and circumstance, the mother clings to her child with an intensity of affection, a devotedness of soul, and a forgetfulness of self, which no other object can call forth. In India this feeling is comparatively weak, and a very slight pretext is sufficient to dissolve the obligation when it has become inconvenient. In time of famine, the parent will sell her child without hesitation. The pressure of extreme want may suggest an excuse for this; but there are attendant circumstances which prove that the sacrifice is not severely felt. This is attested by the following fact, related by Mr. Grant, in his valuable paper on the state of society in India:

"In the scarcity of grain which prevailed about Calcutta in the year 1788, a gentleman then high, now still higher in office there, ordered his servants to buy any children that might be brought for

for sale (for in times of dearth Hindoo parents frequently sell their offspring), and to tell their mothers, that when the scarcity should be over, they might come again and receive their children back. Of about twenty thus humanely preserved, most of whom were females, only three were ever inquired for by their mothers. The scarcity was neither extreme nor long. The unnatural parents cannot be supposed to have perished from want, for each received money for her child, and by the liberal contribution of the inhabitants of Calcutta, and chiefly of the Europeans, rice was distributed daily to multitudes at various stations about the city. And yet, notwithstanding this facility of obtaining food, a woman was at that time seen to throw away her infant child upon the high road." Such facts require no comment.

Infanticide was common until forbidden by British law. The horrible practice of suttee has fallen before the same benign influence. Both these customs indicate a people destitute of moral sensibility, and neither of them would have been discontinued but by the interposition of foreign authority.

The absence of the gentler feelings is not compensated by the possession of the loftier sensibilities of our nature. Patriotism is a virtue absolutely unknown. His country is nothing to the Hindoo, whose affections are centered in himself.

The

The coldness and insensibity of the native character might lead to the supposition, that the vices which usually result from the excitement of passion would be of rare occurrence, but the conclusion would be erroneous. India is disgraced by the grossest impurity, which, emanating from the institutions of a false religion, spreads itself through all the ramifications of social life, poisoning the very sources of moral principle, and producing a license, both of action and speech, as odious as it is vile. The tone of conversation is represented as indescribably disgusting, and altogether without parallel in European society, however debased. Females of abandoned character are appendages to the temples of religion, and the corruption of manners is universal. It has been seen that mothers will, without reluctance, sell their children; and, to complete the frightful picture of moral deformity, it may be added, that they will sell them for the vilest purposes. The religion of the Hindoo has no connection with sound morals.

The defects of the Hindoo character are pointed out by Tamerlane in his Institutes. He says, "The inhabitants of Hindostan are equally debilitated in their corporeal and inert in their mental faculties; inexorable and perfidious to such an extreme, that only personal violence can enforce justice. Regardless of honour and indecent in their dress, they sacrifice their

their lives for trifles and are indefatigable in unworthy pursuits. Whilst improvident and imprudent, their ideas are confined and views circumscribed. When reduced to poverty, they patiently have recourse to the most menial employments, forgetting their previous circumstances, and seldom quitting the world without injuring their benefactors; but whilst the acquisition of riches tempers every atrocity, indolence pervades their most momentous transactions. The native of Hindostan has no pretension to humanity but the figure; whilst imposture, fraud, and deception, are by him considered as meritorious accomplishments." The opinion of Tamerlane upon this subject must of course be received with some caution. He was a conqueror, and the disciple of a religion in which bigotry and persecution are virtues. His own character, too, did not peculiarly qualify him to act the part of a moral censor. But after all these deductions from his credibility, considerable weight must be attached to his report, and in all its main features it is corroborated by a host of later testimonies which are perfectly unimpeachable. Bernier, who visited them above a hundred and fifty years ago, speaks of their faithless and perfidious character, and declares his belief that there does not exist a nation more avaricious and sordid. Mr. Scrafton, about the middle of the last century, says, "The Gentoos are found still

more

more cruel and rapacious than their foreign masters, and what is more extraordinary, the Brahmins still exceed the rest in every abuse of power, and seem to think, if they bribe God by bestowing part of their plunder on cows and faquirs, their injustices will be pardoned." Governor Holwell, about the same time, calls them "a race of people, who, from their infancy, are utter strangers to the idea of common faith and honesty;"—"as degenerate, crafty, superstitious, litigious, and wicked a people as any in the known world, if not eminently more so." Lord Clive, who knew them well, says, "The inhabitants of this country we know by long experience have no attachment to an obligation." Governor Verelst, an able and well informed cotemporary of the latter authorities, bears ample testimony to the treachery and dishonesty of the native character. In 1772, the Governor and Council of Bengal complain of the mischievous consequences flowing from the prevalence of litigiousness, chicane, and intrigue. Lord Teignmouth affirms that "the nation is wholly void of public virtue;" that the natives "make not the least scruple of lying when falsehood is attended with advantage"—that "cunning and artifice is wisdom with them—to deceive and overreach is to acquire the character of a wise man"—that "a man must be long acquainted with them before he can believe them

them capable of that barefaced falsehood, servile adulation, and deliberate deception which they daily practise ;"—and that " it is the business of all, from the ryot to the dewan, to conceal and deceive." Sir John Macpherson, adverting to these statements, admits that they " are not fictitious representations." Sir Robert Barker says, " it is well known that neither promises nor oaths have been able to bind this treacherous sect of people to their engagements." Mr. Grant sums up a long and able enquiry into the native character thus: " Upon the whole, then, we cannot avoid recognizing in the people of Hindostan, a race of men lamentably degenerate and base, retaining but a feeble sense of moral obligation, yet obstinate in their disregard of what they know to be right; governed by malevolent and licentious passions, strongly exemplifying the effects produced upon society by great and general corruption of manners, and sunk in misery by their vices in a country peculiarly calculated by its natural advantages to promote the happiness of its inhabitants." The general tendency of the evidence before the parliamentary committee is to the same effect. Mr. Clarke says, " a native will, in general, give his evidence rather with reference to the consequences of what he may say to his own interests, than from any regard to truth or falsehood"—" in order to the improvement of the native

tive character, I think there is wanting a better moral principle in themselves individually than they are now found to possess, and a more powerful influence of moral opinion on the part of native society. At present, their morality affords little internal control over their actions; it does not furnish them with a conscientious check over their conduct, and there is no control of public opinion acting upon them externally. Injustice or misconduct which should prove successful in making the fortune of a native, would attach no disgrace to him in the estimation of his countrymen." The same gentleman states, that prosecutions for perjury are very frequent, and if the criminal "is of a character to which, from rank or caste, any degree of respectability or sanctity attaches, those qualities would not be affected by his punishment in the minds of the natives."—He believes, "that persons holding offices attached to temples, have been viewed with equal reverence and treated with equal deference in regard to their spiritual authority while under actual punishment for perjury," and their conviction has not operated as any stain upon them in native society. Mr. Oldham would not trust the natives to administer justice alone—thinks the acutest among them the most corrupt—that a native cannot trust a native, and among the people there is a decided want of regard to character. This gentleman,

gentleman, who held a judicial station in India, relates the following story:

"A murder had taken place in the district of Moradabad. The thannadar, as is usual in those cases, proceeded to the spot to hold an inquest on the body, and to enquire for witnesses of the fact: he took the evidence of one witness, who deposed that he was present at the time the murder was committed, related circumstantially the number of sword-wounds given, the distance he stood from the deceased, &c. I mean merely to state, that the most minute particulars were given by this man as an eye-witness. The man was summoned before me as a magistrate for his evidence to be taken again. The man's name, as usual, was asked; he gave his name correctly. His father's name was asked; he gave that correctly. He went through the whole circumstances verbatim, as related before the thannadar; but when I began to ask him a little more, and cross-question him a little, he lost himself quite, and seeing that I suspected there was something that there should not be, and followed it up, the man having no answer to give, at last said, 'The whole of the evidence I have given is by order of the zemindar. I am not the real witness, but am come to personate him by the zemindar's orders.'"

The Honourable W. Leslie Melville says: "If all the testimony delivered on the subject of India

dia agrees in any thing, it surely is in representing the low state of moral feeling exhibited in our courts of justice." Native officers and retainers, as well as suitors and witnesses, are all represented as false and corrupt. Mr. Butterworth Bayley says: "The great cause of failure in the administration of criminal, as well as of civil justice, is the habitual disregard for truth which unhappily pervades the bulk of the native community, and the little security which the obligation of an oath adds to the testimony of a witness. I do not believe that this characteristic vice of the natives of India has been fostered or encouraged by the establishment of our courts of justice as is generally imagined. The same vice has been found to prevail to at least an equal extent in Mysore, in the Mahratta country, and in other parts of India to which our authority has not extended, and where our institutions were wholly unknown. False testimony has, in certain cases, been directly encouraged and approved by the great lawgiver of the Hindoos; the offence of perjury can be expiated by very simple penances, and *the inhabitants of India must undergo a great moral regeneration*, before the evil which saps the very foundation, of justice, and bars all confidence between man and man, shall be effectually remedied. My own impression is that, generally speaking, the moral sanction of an oath does not, especially

especially among the lower classes, materially add to the value of native testimony; that the only practical restraint on perjury is dread of the punishment prescribed by law for that offence, and that the fear of consequences in a future state, or the apprehended loss of character and reputation among their countrymen, has little effect in securing true and honest testimony on the part of those who may be influenced by fear, favour, or affection." Mr. Holt Mackenzie admits, that the natives regard their own countrymen with distrust. Captain Macan, speaking of the native troops, not only declares them to be, "without any exception, the most gasconading and the vainest race of men" he "had ever met;" but adds his testimony to the universal selfishness. He says, "they talk a good deal about loyalty and honour; but I think, from an intimate knowledge of the native character, they feel only for their own interest." The government has repeatedly added the seal of its confirmation to the universal tendency of individual testimony. As early as 1772, the Governor and Council of Bengal are found complaining of the "litigiousness" of the natives as productive of "endless expense and actual oppression," and expressing an anxiety "to curb and restrain trivial and groundless complaints, and to deter chicane and intrigue, which passions among these people often work to the undoing

undoing of their neighbours." And as late as 1827, the Bengal Government advert to the want of veracity in the natives as matter of notoriety. They say, "it is needless to remark how much the proceedings of all our tribunals are delayed and embarrassed by the notorious disregard for truth, so generally displayed by the natives in giving evidence, and from their want of moral principle, evils *which cannot be mitigated or remedied by any direct or immediate modification of our* JUDICIAL INSTITUTIONS." To multiply such quotations would be easy if it were necessary; but the authorities already adduced are sufficient to attest the moral darkness which envelops India.

The fact cannot be denied, and the important questions are, Whence does it arise? and How is it to be removed? The first question is not to be answered by referring to physical circumstances. That these have some small effect in modifying character may be true; but with the page of universal history before us, we cannot attribute the great distinctions of national character to physical causes. How different the ancient Romans from the modern Italians, though placed in the same physical circumstances. Who would recognize the descendants of the conquerors of the world in the men who exist but to languish at an opera, or flutter at a masquerade? The mere difference of race will not account for this; for though

though on the old Roman stock some barbarian shoots have been engrafted, it must be remembered that the northern hordes who pressed into the fair provinces of the south, during the decline of the Roman empire, were as brave, as hardy, and as warlike, as those whose domains they invaded. That national character changes without any foreign admixture, and though the soil and climate remain unaltered, we have abundant proof, and the change does not always require any great lapse of time. Events sometimes take place, of so stirring a nature, as to perform the work of centuries in a few years. Every instance which history furnishes of national degeneracy or national advancement, is a proof of the efficiency of moral causes, and the comparative inertness of physical circumstances.

We must not, then, conclude that the vices of the Hindoo character are the result of his enervating climate. The slightest consideration, indeed, must shew us the falsehood of such a conclusion, since the variations of the climate are considerable, and those of national character very slight, those slight variations being capable of being accounted for from moral causes, and from moral causes alone. We must search for more substantial reasons for the lamentable state in which we find the people of India; and it would not appear unreasonable to ascribe some of their vices to the

misfortune

misfortune of their civil position. A long course of bondage may be allowed to have some influence in deadening the moral sensibilities, and raising an abundant crop of all the meaner vices. The dictum of the Greek philosopher, that the hour that makes a man a slave deprives him of half his value, might have been illustrated in their history; and, judging from their present character, we might suspect such to be the fact. Lying is especially the vice of slaves. Violence and oppression call forth deceit to counteract them. The victim of despotism feels that he has no other resource; and he has no self-respect to restrain him from the employment of that which he regards as his only protection. Where the same practice is indulged by all, it is, of course, unaccompanied by shame in any. Infamy does not follow detection. After a time there will be no attempt at concealment, except from the common enemy; and at last, a proficiency in falsehood will be accounted the highest proof of genius. Dishonesty is another natural consequence of political slavery, as it is the natural associate of mendacity. Where the ruler will, if possible, take all, the subject will, of course, preserve as much as he can. As the law will not protect him, he will endeavour to protect himself; but he will not long stop here; he will not long preserve two measures of justice—one for his ruler and one for his

his fellow-subjects. He will soon learn to deal with the latter as with the former; he will come to regard society as the scene of an universal scramble, in which every one must take all he can get, and he will sedulously follow the example of his master, in drawing to himself as much treasure as possible, without regard to the means of acquisition. Malevolence and cruelty are further consequences of a state of political oppression. The brave are usually humane; but the cowardice which attends subjection disposes men to cruelty. The spirit which dare not resist, will yet burn to revenge; such a feeling, long indulged, will, of course, gather strength, and the desire of vengeance will become co-extensive with the belief of injury. These results will be greatly accelerated, if the rules of justice should be relaxed, not only between the state and the subject, but also between man and man. If the privilege of oppression and plunder should not be confined to the ruling authorities, but, through the corruption of courts of justice, sold to all who have the power of purchasing it, the progress of demoralization will be rapid indeed. Dishonesty will have free range, and every accession of plunder will increase the power of making fresh ones. Malevolence will possess unbounded means of gratification, and the law will be an engine of persecution as ready as it is powerful. In this

state

state of things, falsehood will be at a premium, inasmuch as it will be a constant and unfailing instrument, whether of cupidity or of revenge. That the Hindoos were oppressed and plundered by their Mahomedan conquerors, is certain; that the courts of justice, under those rulers, were corrupt, almost beyond conception, is equally so. And we might be justified in ascribing the demoralization of the people to some such process as that which has been described, were there not reason to believe that, previously to their subjection by the Moguls, they were in a state no better than that in which they were found at the breaking up of the empire of the conquerors. The question, too, occurs, How came a people, so numerous and powerful, to fall so readily into the power of strangers, possessing no extraordinary advantages for successful invasion? It is obvious that one part of the national character must then have been precisely what it is now. There must have been the same want of public spirit and patriotic feeling; the same absence of all regard for the common good; the same centralisation of the entire feelings of the man in self. From despotism they might have suffered, but that despotism was a domestic one. To what cause, then, shall we attribute that prostration of mind and depravity of heart which have sunk a great people into wretchedness, and rendered them the object of political contempt and of moral abhorrence? The answer is readily obtained—to superstition; to the prevalence of a mighty system of religious imposture, as atrocious as it is extravagant; which, in the same degree that it dishonours the Supreme Being, corrupts and debases his rational creatures; which, upon the most outrageous absurdity engrafts the most abominable vice, and rears a temple to false and filthy deities upon the ruins of human intellect and human virtue. It were criminal to conceal or palliate the real cause of Hindoo degeneracy. It is false religion, and nothing beside.

The gods whom the Hindoos worship are impersonations of all the vices and all the crimes which degrade human nature; and there is no grossness and no villainy which does not receive countenance from the example of some or other of them. The vilest and most scandalous impurity pervades their mythology throughout; is interwoven with all its details; is at once its groundwork and completion; its beginning and its end. The robber has his god, from whom he invokes a blessing on his attempts against the life and property of his neighbour. Revenge, as well as robbery, finds a kindred deity; and cruelty, the never-failing companion of idolatry, is of the essence of the system.

The rites and ceremonies are worthy of the faith;

faith; they may be summed up in three words, folly, licentiousness, and cruelty. Penances, silly and revolting, are the means of expiating sin. Grossness the most horrible, both in nature and in degree, from which the most abandoned characters in the most abandoned parts of Europe would recoil, enters into public worship, and the higher festivals are honoured by an increased measure of profligacy. That unhappy class of females, who every where else are regarded with contemptuous scorn, or with painful commiseration, are in India appendages to the temples of religion. The Hindoo faith, in perfect conformity with its character, demands barbarous as well as licentious exhibitions and torture, and death are among its acceptable modes of service.

From such deities and such modes of worship, what can we expect but what we find? If the sublime example of perfect purity, which true religion places before its followers, be calculated to win to virtue, must not universal contamination be the necessary consequence of investing pollution and crime with the garb of divinity? If men find licentiousness and cruelty associated with the ceremonies of religion, is it possible that they should believe them to be wrong? Can they be expected in private life to renounce as criminal, practices which in public they have been taught to regard as meritorious? Will they abhor in the

world

world that which they reverence in the sanctuary? It were absurd to believe it.

A false religion engenders a spurious morality. In the Hindoo code of duty, "the weightier matters of the law" scarcely find place. Almsgiving is inculcated; but it is in behalf of a tribe of proud, lazy, sturdy mendicants, to whom almsgiving is not charity. But the great points of Hindoo morality consist in ceremonial observances, burdensome as they are idle. Surrounded on all sides by danger, the votary of this impious superstition can scarcely move or refrain from motion without incurring defilement. Ablutions and purifications, prohibitions of certain kinds of food, and regulations for dressing that which is permitted; minute directions for all the most indifferent actions of life—these swell the interminable list of empty forms, which excuse the absence of purity, justice, and charity.

The Hindoo system prescribes the observance of frivolous ceremonies, and neglects to inculcate important moral duties. But its pernicious influence does not terminate there: it enforces much that is positively evil. By the institution of castes it estranges man from his fellows, and shuts up the avenues of benevolence; invests one part of society with the privilege of unrestrained indulgence—casting over them the cloak of sanctity, however unworthy—shielding them from the consequences

sequences of their actions, however flagitious; and condemns another to hopeless and perpetual debasement, without the chance of emancipation or improvement. A system more mischievous or iniquitous—better calculated to serve the interests of vice, or destroy those of virtue—seems beyond the power of the most perverted ingenuity to frame. The root being corrupt, so are the branches. Precepts are given, which set at nought all the first principles of morality. False testimony is distinctly permitted in a number of specified cases, some of which are sufficiently ludicrous did the subject admit of mirth. The profession of a robber is recognised as a lawful one, by giving a rule for the division of the spoil. Punishments of the last degree of barbarity are denounced against atrocious crimes, against crimes of no very deep malignity, and against actions that are no crimes at all. Falsehood, fraud, and cruelty are thus directly sanctioned, and the numerous rules relating to another branch of morals, many of them trifling, many licentious, and all of them disgusting, are quite sufficient to account for the laxity which exists in practice. Such are the sources of Hindoo morality, and the connection between cause and effect is illustrated by the state of society. The religion and its ceremonies, the code and its precepts, naturally lead to the expectation that the disciples of such a religion, the subjects of such a code, would be precisely what all report represents the natives of India as being.

But the dominion of superstition, though long is not eternal, and the mists in which the mind of India has been so long enveloped are already beginning to clear away. How this good work may be best advanced is a most interesting and important enquiry. Much importance is attached to education, and its influence is not to be despised; but an education which left the people as morally depraved as it found them, would scarcely be preferable to none. Yet instruction, in mere human learning, may do much in preparing the way for the reception of a far more valuable species of knowledge. It may break down prejudices; it may shew to this long-deluded people the absurdity of their own faith, and lead them to feel the want of a better. This operation has begun: motion has commenced in the long slumbering mass, and it will go on increasing in strength, until the idols before which the intellect of India has been prostrated, shall be hurled from their pedestals, amidst the applauses of those who once bowed before them in slavish adoration.

The symptoms of this agitation are too evident to be mistaken. Mr. Lushington says: " Some of the students, who have completed their education in the Hindoo college and other institutions, are in the habit of holding debating societies, where they

they discuss topics of considerable importance in the English language, and read lectures and essays of their own composition upon various literary and scientific subjects. At one of the meetings above-mentioned the question was, 'Whether posthumous fame be a rational principle of human action or not?' It is true, that the debate soon branched off into a consideration of the possibility and probability of human perfection; but the orators spoke with remarkable fluency, quoting Gibbon, Hume, Reid, Bolingbroke, Voltaire, Shakespear, Milton, &c. The forms of similar meetings in England were imitated; and the chairman having inquired the reason of the secretary's absence, a loud cry of 'Persecution!' was raised, and it was explained that he was prevented by his father, who was afraid that his principles of paganism should be corrupted in consequence of the other members being deists. Thus has the beginning of a most wonderful change been worked among a race, who for a long time were considered as sunk in a hopeless state of ignorance and the blindest idolatry. I should have mentioned before, that one of the young Hindoos in question, being called upon at the police to swear, as usual, on the waters of the Ganges, declined, averring, that he should just as soon swear by the waters of the Nile." It thus appears that there is some danger of deism becoming the popular

popular faith. Of the authors mentioned by Mr. Lushington as familiar to the Hindoo students, four out of seven are advocates of deistical opinions. And Mr. Sherer states, that a large impression of Paine's works, which arrived in Calcutta from America, was eagerly bought up by the Hindoo youths, who had received instruction in English. Even among the Brahmins deism is making progress, and some opposition to Christian schools has arisen from this source. Bishop Heber says, "Our chief hindrances are some deistical Brahmins, who have left their old religion, and desire to found a sect of their own." This is not, indeed, precisely the course of events which the friends of religion would desire; but it is not, upon the whole, discouraging. It may even be considered as a favourable symptom. The acknowledgment of the first great article of all true religion, may be a preparation for the reception of the remainder. When a nation, which has heretofore maintained a belief in revelation, rejects it, as the French did, forty years ago, in favour of the cold dogmas of a corrupted deism, it is a fearful shadow of "coming events," and may justify an apprehension that the light which that country has enjoyed is about to be extinguished altogether. The abandonment even of a corrupted form of Christianity, must be a change for the worse. But when a nation casts "to the moles and the

bats"

bats" a system of idolatry so absurd and so horrible as that of the Hindoos, even though mere deism be substituted, it is a step in advance. Something is gained by the recognition of one Supreme Being; and on this foundation we should not despair of raising the sublime superstructure of Christianity. In this way, human knowledge will act as the pioneer of religious truth. It must not be looked to as an efficient instrument for effecting the moral reformation of the people. It is too often so regarded, not only with respect to India, but to other countries. This is an error. Human knowledge is incapable of purifying the heart; it does not address itself to this object, and its most judicious advocates will make no such pretensions on its behalf; it has not even a direct influence in promoting the interests either of virtue or piety, though its diffusion in a country situated like India tends indirectly to these purposes. The light of knowledge will shew the Hindoo the folly of his old superstitions; and as these are the great sources of his demoralization, something will be gained by their destruction. Human knowledge will be admirably useful in pulling down; but another species of knowledge, far higher and more valuable, will be necessary to build up. We should therefore promote, by all the means in our power, the diffusion of genuine science and sound learning in our Indian possessions;

sions; but if we stop here, we do little. We should regard this only as a means to an end, and that end the establishment of the only system of religious belief which can render men either virtuous in this world or happy in another.

Experience justifies us in expecting benefit from such a course. Christianity has advanced most rapidly in countries enlightened by science, and refined by elegant literature. Among barbarous and uncivilized nations its progress has been comparatively slow. It may not be that in any country the most learned have been the earliest in embracing it; but in every place where knowledge exists, except it be confined by pains and penalties to a peculiar class, its benefits extend far beyond the circle of philosophers, and where freedom of enquiry is permitted, the leaven of thought will gradually pervade the whole mass. The gospel was first proclaimed in one of the most polished ages of the world—when the conquering arms of Rome had been the means of spreading the arts, the knowledge, and the civilization which she herself had received from Greece, over every part of her mighty empire; and it was in the most refined and inquisitive portions of that empire—it was in Asia Minor and Italy, that the progress of conversion was the most rapid and successful. Ignorance on the contrary, is favourable to error. The impostor Mahomet commenced

menced his career in an age when the lustre of Grecian and Roman civilization had been dimmed by the operation of various causes—when that cloud which hung for centuries over the human mind, was enlarging in circumference and deepening in blackness ; and while Christianity had triumphed over the gods of ancient times by moral means alone, Mahomet owed his success to the keenness, not of his arguments, but of his sword. With these facts before us, we may conclude that knowledge and civilization are favourable to the progress of truth, and to the operation of moral causes, and in this belief we may regard the introduction of the sciences and learning of the west among the Hindoos with pleasure and with confidence. Our religion will follow and accomplish that "great moral regeneration," the necessity for which has been so forcibly urged by one of the ablest of Indian statesmen. The Hindoos have been debased by a false religion; they must be restored to a healthy state of moral feeling by the true one. All other remedies will be at best but miserable palliatives—this alone will go to the root of the disease.

What then is to be done to promote this end? By direct means scarcely any thing. We cannot divert any large portion of the funds of India to the purpose—the state of the revenue will not bear it; and if it would, the natives would probably

bably view such an appropriation with a degree of dislike which would not only impair our influence, but what is of far greater importance, retard the reception of revealed truth. Government can do little except by encouraging education. The system of education at present must be in a considerable degree irrespective of religion; but there is no necessity for discouraging the reading of the sacred volume. Nothing should be done which is likely to induce parents to withdraw their children from the schools; but the Scriptures may be read like any other books, and experience shews that the natives regard this neither with distaste nor apprehension. The moral influence of the children thus educated in the families to which they belong, is a point not to be overlooked: in many instances, the parents have regarded with approbation the books which the scholars carried home from school, and especially the New Testament. The schools are also beneficial in breaking down the distinctions of caste. At first, some attempts may be made to preserve these distinctions, but they soon cease, and the children of various castes mix together upon a footing of equality.

One most unexceptionable mode of advancing the cause of Christianity is, by the example of those who profess to believe it. If they display indifference to the religion in which they have been

been educated, there is but slender hope of conciliating the respect of the Hindoo towards a faith which neither he nor his fathers have known. Obedience should be yielded not only to the moral precepts of Christianity, but also to its positive institutions. The Christian festival of Sunday should command that decent respect to which it is entitled. In a few instances, it is to be regretted, that the magistrates and revenue officers do not close their courts on that day. This is certainly wrong, and ought to be amended. There would, indeed, be little difficulty in procuring a general observance of Sunday, as the Hindoos and Mahometans mutually keep each other's festivals, and in such a climate as that of India, an invitation to rest could scarcely be unpopular.

Although both state and christian policy restrain us from maintaining a religious establishment commensurate with the moral wants of the people, we ought to make sufficient provision for the spiritual instruction and consolation of those Christians who are called to reside in a country where Paganism is yet the dominant creed. This has not always been attended to. For many years the number of chaplains was lamentably small. It has been increased, and the good effects which have followed have justified the propriety of the increase. Several, however, of the witnesses before the Parliamentary Committee

regard

regard even the present number as quite inadequate. For a long period the English church in India was without the superintendence of a Bishop. This is not a place for religious controversy, and it is not intended to enquire what form of church government is most apostolic; but certainly an episcopal church without a bishop is an anomaly which could not have existed at any previous period since the promulgation of Christianity. Dr. Buchanan relates, that a Syrian bishop, with whom he conversed, thought it strange that there was no bishop in India to superintend so large an empire, and said that he did not perfectly comprehend our ecclesiastical principles. The difficulty might well perplex him; but, at length, principally through the exertions of Dr. Buchanan, the anomaly was removed by the erection of the see of Calcutta. But the slighest reflection will show that a single bishop for the whole of the British possessions in India is altogether inadequate. By the late act, the King has power to create two new bishoprics, Madras and Bombay, and to assign to the three dioceses their respective limits. This provision has not yet been acted upon; but when put in force it will make an important addition to the efficiency of the English church in India.

No inconsiderable proportion of the British residents in India being natives of the northern part

part of this island, the late act properly provides that the Company shall maintain, at each of the presidencies, two chaplains of the Church of Scotland. This clause contains a provision of which the policy, and even the intention, is by no means clear. It is the following: "Provided always, That nothing herein contained shall be so construed as to prevent the Governor General in Council from granting from time to time, with the sanction of the Court of Directors and of the Commissioners for the Affairs of India, to any sect, persuasion, or community of Christians not being of the United Church of England and Ireland, or of the Church of Scotland, such sums of money as may be expedient for the purpose of Instruction, or for the maintenance of Places of Worship." This strange provision is happily only permissive. The Government are not restrained from thus granting money; but it is to be hoped that they will restrain themselves. To act upon this provision would be to open a door which, in a short time, it would be found impossible to close. To recognise the claims of one sect, would embolden all others to assert their's. No distinction could be drawn, that would not give serious, and perhaps reasonable, offence to those who were excluded by it, whilst an unlimited compliance would drain the resources of India, excite serious dissatisfaction in the minds of the natives, and prove a stumbling-block in the way of Christianity. A moderate provision is made for the Protestant Episcopal, and Presbyterian churches; and this is justified by the circumstance of their being established in the two divisions of the protecting country. The majority of European residents will belong to one of these churches. Those who do not, will generally be members of one of the denominations of Protestant Dissenters, and such will feel no scruple in attending the worship of the church of Scotland. But it must not be forgotten, that the provision thus made is the exception, not the rule; and that very weighty reasons forbid such exceptions to be multiplied.

But though we cannot do any thing directly to promote the success of missionary exertions, it is a solemn duty to abstain from doing any thing to impede them. Every denomination of Christian missionaries should be permitted freely to use their own resources, in the manner which appears to them best adapted to promote their peculiar views of the doctrines of religion. Two things are especially desirable in those who undertake the important task of unfolding to the natives the discoveries of revelation—discretion and charity. By cultivating these, they will advance their common end far more than lies in the power of government to promote it by pecuniary assistance.

As

As no impediment should be thrown in the way of conversion, so no disability should be incurred in consequence of it. This is so clear, that it may seem scarcely necessary to announce it. But unfortunately, native Christians have been excluded, on account of their faith, from offices to which Hindoos and Mahometans were eligible. This evil, it may be presumed, is corrected by that clause of the last act, which declares, that no native or natural-born subject of his Majesty "shall, by reason only of his *religion*, place of birth, descent, or colour, or any of them, be disabled from holding office under the Company." Some difficulties have been suggested as to inheritance of property by converts to Christianity. If such exist, they ought to be removed. Men should not be seduced into the profession of Christianity by the temptation of temporal benefit, but they certainly ought not to be deterred from embracing it by the prospect of penalty and loss.

Nothing can be plainer than that converts should be protected from persecution; from the necessity of complying with practices which their consciences disapprove; and from all inconveniences, pecuniary or otherwise, resulting from their change of faith. Another point, equally clear, is, that the neutrality of government should be perfect. While, on the one hand, it should not force Christianity on the people, on the other, it it should on no account evince any appearance of approbation towards idolatry.

The government formerly drew a portion of its revenue from a source, the propriety of which was much questioned. A certain sum per head was collected upon all pilgrims resorting to the great temples, and to those smaller pagodas which had acquired celebrity, and the offerings which the devotees brought with them were likewise subjected to a toll. Sums were also levied for permission to perform the various ridiculous and revolting acts of penance, and for licenses to erect shops, booths, and stalls, for the accommodation of those who resorted to the festivals. These sources of revenue have been recently abandoned, and, of course, will never be revived; but the question of their continuance was agitated with great zeal and ingenuity. It was, indeed, one which it was by no means easy to answer satisfactorily. To acquire income from so abominable a source, seems, at first sight, even more reprehensible than the French practice of deriving a revenue from licensing places of vicious indulgence. But, in order to make the cases parallel, it must be supposed that we have the power, consistently with our avowed toleration of the Hindoo religion, to suppress these idolatrous practices altogether. On the other hand, the pilgrim tax has been compared to a duty upon ardent spirits, by which the

the consumption of an article pernicious to health and morals is diminished; but the comparison is not just. The use of ardent spirits is not unlawful in itself—it is the excess only that is criminal. But idolatry is unlawful in all forms and all degrees. At the same time, the suggestion that the only effect of the abolition of the tax would be a great increase in the number of worshippers, as the means would be placed within the power of many who before were excluded by the cost, was certainly entitled to attention. The question was, undoubtedly, one altogether of great difficulty, and which reflecting and well-principled men would generally be found to answer with hesitation. If by retaining the tax, we were understood as giving any sanction to the abominations of idolatry, we were doing great wrong both to our Hindoo fellow-subjects and ourselves. If by abolishing it we have extended the practices which we are most desirous to suppress, we have done harm in another way. In such circumstances, even an honest intention affords little security for a sound conclusion, and the event only will enable us to judge accurately of the measure.

The earliest Christian church established in India was that of the Syrian Christians, which is said to trace its origin to St. Thomas. For many years they appear to have met with considerable success among the Brahmins and Nairs of Travancore,

core, who compose the military caste, and are the nobility of that country. They were protected by the reigning government, and enjoyed the same privileges as the other inhabitants. About the middle of the sixteenth century they were disturbed by the appearance of Roman Catholics in the province, who are alleged to have destroyed many of their public records, church formularies, and copies of the scriptures. Certain it is that the Catholics, by some means, succeeded in severing from the Syrian church about one-half of its members, and uniting them with their own. The converts, however, though formally attached to the Roman communion, still retained some of their own customs. The Syrian church in Travancore is accordingly at this day separated into two divisions, one called Syrian Christians, and the other Roman Syrians. The former continued in a very depressed state until a few years ago, when Lieutenant-colonel Munro, the British resident at the court of Travancore, interposed on their behalf. In consequence of his representations, many of their former privileges were restored to them; and, under his auspices, a college was established for the education of their clergy, which was supported by a grant of land bestowed for the express purpose by the ranee of Travancore. The exertions of Colonel Munro did not terminate with the establishment of this college.

lege. He obtained the co-operation of some missionaries of the Church of England, under whose care the college was placed, with the entire concurrence of the Syrian bishop, and procured a translation of the scriptures into the vernacular tongue. The number of Syrian Christians is about 70,000; that of the Roman Syrians is about the same. These have a college at Verapoly, under the care of a bishop. The present superintendent is a native of Ireland, educated in Spain.

The professed Catholics were formerly numerous, but by the acknowledgment of their own missionaries their numbers have been certainly decreasing for the last century; and there is reason to believe that many of the conversions of which they boasted were but nominal. The Abbé Dubois has endeavoured to account for the ill success of the Roman missionaries, and the first cause which he assigns for it is the Pope's interference with the practices of the Jesuits. The members of this order, never very scrupulous in the means they employed for the accomplishment of their objects, conformed to many of the idolatrous and superstitious customs of the Hindoos, in order, as they alleged, to conciliate their minds and lead them to embrace the Catholic faith. This was analogous to their conduct in China, where, finding that the fact of the founder of the

Christian

Christian faith having suffered as a malefactor was a cause of offence, they thought fit to deny it, and to affirm that it was a false and malignant report, invented by the Jews and other enemies of Christianity. The members of those orders which retained a less pliant morality were not, however, prepared to follow such examples. The Capuchins, the Jansenists, and others, objected to the vicious conformity of the Jesuits, and appealed to the Pope. His decision was against the practice complained of; but as the Jesuits, though always professing the most unbounded reverence for the Holy See, were far from being the most obedient of its servants, it required repeated remonstrances from Rome to induce them to desist. The fact that such practices were adopted, as lures to the profession of the Christian name, is quite sufficient to shew the character of a large portion, if not the whole, of the alleged converts. The Abbé Dubois, belonging to the Propaganda Society, is, of course, the advocate of the forbidden practices, and regards the decision of the head of the Roman church as having mainly contributed to the decline of the Catholic religion in India. But it is obvious that nothing was lost but in name. A mass of actual Pagans were called Christians; theyare now no longer called so. Their numbers have ceased to swell the roll of Catholic converts; but the genuine interests of Christianity are certainly not injuriously

juriously affected by the change. But the Abbé is not content that the entire blame of retarding the progress of Roman Catholic profession should rest upon the head of his spiritual father. He assigns as a farther cause, the wars between the English and the French. These wars, during their continuance, must have interfered in some degree with the labours of missionaries of every religious profession; but it is certain that the Protestants were, in many parts, far more exposed to suffer from them than the Catholics, and since their cessation the field has been open alike to the labours of both. The last of the three causes which the Abbé Dubois enumerates was, doubtless, a very efficient one. Some of the most zealous of the Roman missionaries endeavoured to recommend themselves to the natives by imposture, and the Hindoos detected it. The Jesuits announced themselves as Brahmins from a distant country, and thereby gained for their persons and their office a degree of respect far surpassing that which they could have hoped for as Europeans, and the propagators of an unknown faith. The consequence was that which always follows unsuccessful imposture—the artifices used were injurious to the cause which they were intended to promote. The Jesuits, who at first were venerated as something more than saints, were afterwards despised as convicted impostors, and the faith

faith which they had disgraced shared in their personal unpopularity. From the ill success of his own church, the Abbé is led to regard all attempt at conversion as hopeless; but the success which has attended missionaries of another kind warrants a different conclusion.

The first Protestant missionary was Bartholomew Ziegenbaly, who was sent to Tranquebar by the king of Denmark in the early part of the last century. Finding himself in want of further protection than his own sovereign could afford him, he came to England, where he was introduced to George the First, and shortly afterwards returned to India, under the patronage of the king and of the bishops of the English church. He was followed by other Lutheran missionaries, among whom the venerable Swartz must not be forgotten. This apostolic man commanded the esteem alike of every description of residents in India, Hindoos, Mahometans, and Europeans. The sovereign of Tanjore, when dying, was anxious to make him the guardian of his heir, a trust which he declined. Hyder Ali received him as an envoy on the part of the English, and offered to take his word as the guarantee of a proposed engagement, when he would trust no one else. On two occasions during war, his character saved the garrison and people in the fort of Tanjore from perishing by famine. There was grain in the country; but the

the people refused to furnish bullocks to carry it, because they had formerly been defrauded of their pay. In this extremity the Rajah applied to Swartz, and that which the credit of the government could not command, was readily obtained on the promise of an humble foreigner, destitute of property, and whose income afforded him only a bare subsistence. These missionaries continued to propagate christianity with considerable success, and a body of Christians, the fruits of their labours, are scattered over India south of Madras; their chief stations being Vepery, Tanjore, Tranquebar, Trichinopoly, Madura, Tinnevelly, Ramnad, and Cuddalore. The number of these Christians it is not easy to estimate; but it is both large and increasing. The amount of increase at one station, Tinnevelly, has been ascertained, and is most encouraging. In 1823 the native Christians in that province were only 4000; they now exceed 8,000. In the south of that province are two villages entirely christian, and from which every vestige of idolatry has disappeared. Bishop Heber, who visited Tanjore and Trichinopoly, was greatly interested in the Christians whom he found in those provinces, and those who have visited Tinnevelly and other parts have been impressed in the same favourable manner by the character of the Christian communities which they met with. The Hindoo tehsildar of the district which contains

contains the two Christian villages already mentioned, when questioned by the visitor, testified to the quiet and inoffensive character of the inhabitants, and said that he should rejoice if all around him resembled them. The mission which has produced such beneficial effects has been supported from its commencement by the English Society for promoting Christian Knowledge.

The progress of Christianity in India is not to be judged altogether by the actual number of converts. The number of these would have been much larger had the missionaries exercised less caution in receiving them. No temporal inducements have been offered to the profession of Christianity; and none are admitted to baptism until after a long probation. The apparent progress is thus rendered slow: but this is counterbalanced by the assurance that outward conformity is a sign of internal conviction, and that those who forsake their old religion are real and not merely nominal converts. In the mean time, the knowledge of the great truths of revelation is spreading far and wide, and where so many hear, some will be convinced.

The Church Missionary Society has, from its establishment, directed a large portion of its attention to India, and sedulously and usefully co-operated with the labourers whom it found already there. Its schools and stations are numerous,

merous, and the number of scholars in the former increased in seven years from 6,581 to 12,298. A lady, under the patronage of this society, succeeded in introducing female schools, in opposition to the prejudices of the natives, which led them to regard the instruction of females with dislike. The excellent and exemplary Baptist Missionaries have done much to advance the interests both of religion and learning, but the number of labourers is yet inadequate to the promised harvest. The worn-out superstition is obviously falling to pieces, to be replaced, either by what is called the religion of nature, or by a better faith, to which that may form a stepping-stone. It is for those who take an interest in the diffusion of Christian knowledge, to consider whether we ought not to avail ourselves of the moral movement, and give it the best direction; and whether the duty of extending the knowledge of divine truth is not especially pressed upon us, as well by the state of opinion and feeling in India, as by the position in which we stand towards that country.

CHAPTER X.

THE JUDICIAL SYSTEM.

THE judicial system of India has hitherto been of a most heterogeneous character, and it must probably continue so for a period of which the duration cannot be anticipated. The law of the Hindoos is founded upon their religion. It is, of course, in many respects, barbarous and absurd. It is also sometimes extremely vague, and, on the whole, very imperfect. The Mahometans introduced their law, which like that of the Hindoos, was closely connected with their religion. The settlement of the British created a necessity for the introduction of a system of law differing from either. The law of England thus obtained a footing in India; but it did not altogether supersede either of the systems which it found previously in operation. But the Hindoo and Mahometan codes were such as no European people could consent to administer; they were, therefore, modified in practice, and while their leading principles were adhered to, their more barbarous provisions were softened or rejected. Circumstances

stances also continually arose to shew the necessity of some additional rules for the administrastration of justice; and the governments of India, from time to time, enacted various Regulations, which, unless annulled by the authorities at home, have the force of law. The principles of judicial administration in India are consequently derived from no fewer than from four different sources, the institutions of the Hindoos, those of the Mahometans, the English law, and the Regulations of the Indian governments. It seems to be the prevailing opinion, that from the wide differences of these various codes, from the general character of the people, from the diversity of languages, and from other causes, the administration of justice has been far from perfect.

The law of England is administered in courts established by royal charter, and called Supreme Courts. Of these there are three; one at Calcutta, composed of a chief justice and two puisne judges; one at Madras, and one at Bombay, composed respectively of a chief justice and one puisne judge. Formerly the regulations of the Indian governments, which were intended to take effect within the jurisdiction of these courts, were required to be registered in them. By the late act, registration is declared no longer necessary to give validity to the regulations of the Governor General in Council, and the power of legislation previously

previously enjoyed by the governments of the other presidencies is withdrawn.

The Supreme Courts exercise jurisdiction over the European population generally, and under certain circumstances over natives also. In this respect their jurisdiction is understood to be restricted within certain local limits; but they have, in some instances, claimed authority over natives residing beyond those limits, on the ground of constructive inhabitancy; and over landed property to a very wide extent, on the ground that the unmoveable estates of all who are personally subject to them, are also within their jurisdiction. They have directed their receiver to manage the collections of very considerable estates in the interior, and thus have, in fact, rendered the whole of the tenantry liable to the process of the Court. On the principle of constructive residence, a trader residing without the limits, but having commercial dealings within them, may be rendered subject to the jurisdiction of the Court. These vague and uncertain claims of jurisdiction ought to be set at rest, especially as the natives entertain a great dislike to the Supreme Courts. Possibly the expense of their proceedings may be a principal source of their objection. English law is not a very cheap commodity at home, and in India it can hardly be expected at a lower rate than in the original market. This, in the eyes of a native, a native, would stamp the system as one of the worst that could possibly exist. Litigation is with him a great luxury, and to make it dear is regarded as an act of oppression. At the same time it must be allowed, that the members of the Supreme Courts cannot possess much knowledge of the native habits and character, nor any familiarity with the native languages; and under these circumstances, it would be well that some considerable limitations should be put upon their jurisdiction.

Previously to the passing of the last Act, the authority of the Supreme Courts was almost paramount to that of the Government; but by that act the Governor General in Council is empowered to make laws and regulations for all courts of justice, whether established by his Majesty's charter or otherwise; but he cannot abolish any of the former description without the previous sanction of the Court of Directors. This sanction must, of course, be subject to the approval of the Board of Control, though the clause does not specify this provision.

The Company's Courts are numerous, and have, at different times, been subject to various modifications. In Bengal, the lowest court of civil judicature is that of the Moonsiff. This is a native officer, who has original jurisdiction in cases where both parties are natives; to a certain amount, without

without appeal, and to a higher amount, subject to the right of appeal to the Zillah Court. He receives no salary, but is paid the amount of the stamp duty taken in lieu of the institution fees on the suits decided. No great care seems to be taken to ensure a due measure of qualification in these officers; and it is represented that, without the protection of appeal, in all cases but suits for very small sums, little confidence would be placed in their decisions.

The Zillah Court, which is the court of appeal from the Moonsiff and some other subordinate authorities, to be noticed hereafter, has also an original jurisdiction to a limited amount. The zillah judge is an European; his decisions, in the first instance, are subject to appeal, and those given in his appellate character, to a special appeal. Each judge is assisted by two native law officers, a Hindoo pundit and a Mahometan moolavie, who act as his assessors, and give opinions on points of native law. These officers also exercise a direct judicial power, as sudder aumeens. In this character they try causes of limited amount, referred to them by the judge. They may further, at the discretion of the judge, hear appeals from the moonsiffs. If the assistance of the two native law-officers is found insufficient, other natives may be appointed to the office of sudder aumeen, according to the wants of the service.

service. Further, each court has, or had (for considerable changes are in progress), one or more European officers, denominated registrars, invested with authority to try causes of a certain class, remitted to them by the judge, and, in certain cases, to hear appeals. It has been proposed to abolish the office of registrar; to create a number of special sudder aumeens, or native judges, of higher rank than previously existed; and to assign to them the duty of determining suits for much larger sums than generally fell under the cognizance of the registrars, as well as that of hearing appeals from the ordinary sudder aumeens. This proposal has been, to a certain extent, acted upon, and the trial of cases in the first instance is now almost wholly in the hands of native judges, their power of jurisdiction being increased to an amount which very few causes in India exceed.

Above the zillah or district courts were the provincial courts, whose authority, as their name implies, extended over a wider circuit. They had an original jurisdiction from the point where that of the zillah court stopped, extending to a much higher amount, and they also heard and decided appeals from the courts below. It is proposed gradually to abolish these courts.

Superior to these is the court of Sudder Dewanny and Nizamut Adawlut. To this court are referred all cases in which the judges may differ

 from

from their law officers; it has the power of calling for and revising the proceedings of any of the courts, and may suspend from office the judges of the provincial and zillah courts. Suits of large amount are sometimes tried originally in this court, but its jurisdiction is chiefly appellate. Its decision is final in all cases, except where the decree appealed against is for a larger sum than £5,000, in which case an appeal lies to the King in council. There was formerly a single court of Sudder Dewanny and Nizamut Adawlut for the presidency, consisting of five judges; but it has been determined to confine the jurisdiction of this court to the lower provinces, and to establish another for the western provinces, consisting of three judges.

The system of judicature in Madras does not essentially differ from that of Bengal before the late changes; but the zillah courts may try original causes to any amount, and suits of any amount may be appealed to the King in council. In Bombay, the judicial arrangements are nearly similar. But there are certain peculiar regulations, in which three different modes are pointed out by which the court may avail itself of native assistance.

The law administered in these courts is chiefly contained in the regulations passed by the respective governments. In suits regarding succession and

and inheritance, as well as marriage, caste, and all other religious usages and institutions, the decisions are governed by the Mahometan law with respect to Mahometans, and the Hindoo law with respect to Hindoos, as expounded by the Mahometan and Hindoo law officers of the court. The pleadings are in writing, and consist, 1st, of the Plaint, which ought to state precisely the matter of complaint and the amount sought to be recovered; 2dly, the Answer; 3dly, the Reply; 4thly, the Rejoinder. If the plaintiff or defendant have omitted any thing material to the suit in the plaint or answer, one supplemental pleading of each kind, but no more, is admitted. The pleadings may be, at the option of the parties, either in Persian, Bengalee, or Hindostanee. The witnesses are examined *vivâ voce* in open court, and the evidence reduced to writing in one of the languages just mentioned. The causes are conducted by native pleaders, called vakeels. They draw the pleadings and examine the witnesses, but it is not customary for them to address the court. Some of these pleaders are said to display considerable acuteness; but the situation is not considered a respectable one, except in the superior courts. The vakeels are appointed by the respective courts, and are liable to be punished for malpractices, by fine or dismissal. The fees of these officers are regulated by law, but the principle of remuneration appears extraordinary. The vakeel receives

receives a per-centage upon the amount claimed, which the suitor is obliged to deposit in court before the pleader does any act. At the close of the suit the amount is paid over to the vakeel, subject to certain deductions, at the discretion of the court, where the case has not been fully proceeded in. On the first 5,000 rupees the vakeel is allowed five per cent. On sums exceeding that amount, a diminished per-centage is allowed, up to 80,000 rupees, beyond which the vakeel's fee is fixed at 1,000 rupees, which it is in no case to exceed. Among the reforms which will, in all probability, be introduced in the practice of Indian judicature, a better method of remunerating the services of the pleader may be anticipated. The duties which he is called upon to perform, when the amount in litigation is large, may often be less difficult and less laborious than those which devolve upon him when the sum contended for is comparatively small. To reward him munificently in the former case, and scantily in the latter, is offering a premium upon idleness and negligence in the conduct of causes of small amount.

A great part of the duties which in this country are performed by attornies, are in India executed by agents, designated mookhtars; but these persons are not recognized by the court, nor are their charges admitted to form part of the legal costs of suit.

The administration of the criminal law in Bengal

gal (with the exception of those duties termed magisterial) was originally confided to the provincial courts. Inconvenience having been found to arise from this arrangement, a new set of functionaries were appointed, under the title of commissioners of revenue and circuit, to whom the entire criminal jurisdiction was transferred. This, however, was found to answer no better than the former plan, and it was thought necessary to make provision for relieving the commissioners from their duties as criminal judges, and to invest with that character the judges of the zillah courts. The functions of magistracy which had been previously exercised by the zillah judges, have, by the new arrangement, been transferred to the collectors. The Court of Sudder Dewanny and Nizamut Adawlut is, in criminal as in civil matters, the highest authority. It is empowered to grant mitigation or remission of punishment; and no sentence of death, transportation, or perpetual imprisonment, is to be carried into execution without a previous revision of the trial by this court. In Madras, the zillah judges and assistant judges try minor offences: the circuit duties are performed by judges of superior rank. It was proposed also to invest the sudder aumeens with limited powers as criminal judges. In Bombay, the criminal law is administered by session judges, and judges of the Sudder Court make an annual circuit of inspection,

spection, with all the powers to revise and correct the proceedings of the judicial officers which were formerly exercised by the Court of Circuit. The collectors exercise a limited judicial authority in criminal cases.

Criminal justice in Bengal is administered upon the principles of the Mahometan law, of course considerably modified by the force of European opinion. In Bombay, the authority of the Mahometan law is renounced, and a written code substituted. The same plan has either been adopted, or is proposed for adoption, in Madras.

The use of the Mahometan law throws considerable power into the hands of the Moslem law officer of the court. When the whole of the evidence has been taken, he delivers his futwah or decision. This includes both the law and the fact; the futwah declaring whether or not the fact is proved, and what the Mahometan law is upon the subject. If the law officer finds the fact proved, and the judge agrees with him, the sentence is carried into execution, if it fall short of death, transportation for life, or perpetual imprisonment. If the judge dissent, the whole trial must be referred to the Sudder. If the law officer finds the fact not proved, the prisoner is forthwith released, unless in extraordinary cases where the judge sees reason to suspect something improper, and takes on himself the responsibility of remitting

remitting the case. Notwithstanding the large discretion thus entrusted to the native officer, it is said that he rarely attempts to give his judgment without indirectly trying to discover the impression of the judge. But with all this habitual deference in the native officers, the position of the European judge, under the circumstances in which he is placed, does not appear the most dignified.

The power of the inferior officers of the court appears to have been further increased by a practice alleged to have been rendered necessary by the pressure of business. In the heavier class of offences tried before the Court of Circuit, the evidence was always delivered in the hearing of the judge; but in the trial of misdemeanors, and smaller offences, this wholesome practice is dispensed with. The evidence is previously taken down, and then the witnesses and prisoner are brought before the judge, who puts such further questions as he thinks necessary.

The Mahometan law of India renders the testimony of two witnesses necessary to conviction. It requires also direct testimony to the fact charged as a criminal offence. The Mahometan law officers, however, contrive to evade this, even in the gravest cases. In a case involving the punishnishment of death, the Moolavie will sometimes convict on circumstantial evidence only, but will

state

state in his futwah that the extreme sentence is barred by the want of direct testimony; and the prisoner will escape death, but be subjected to a minor punishment. This mixing up of the degrees of evidence with the measure of punishment is excessively absurd. The punishment which the law denounces may be too severe for the particular case, and if so it ought to be mitigated. But the mitigation should take place upon proper grounds. The degree of guilt can have nothing to do with the degree of evidence. A light degree of criminality is a ground for a light measure of punishment. An insufficient degree of evidence is a ground for exemption from punishment altogether. The man is either guilty or not guilty. There is no middle stage. If guilty, he ought to be punished according to his deserts; if not guilty, he ought to be acquitted. The law requires direct testimony, and declares that conviction cannot lawfully take place upon any thing short of it. But when direct testimony is not to be had, (and considering how cheaply evidence may be purchased in India, it is seldom wanting where any one has an interest in obtaining it), such is the laudable zeal of the Mahometan interpreters for inflicting punishment, that rather than be disappointed, they will violate the commands of their own law. Yet they have a conscience in their iniquity; they will not put a man to death whom their

their law declares innocent, as far as human judgment can extend; but they will punish him by fine and imprisonment. His life shall be spared, but his liberty and his purse are trifles. It is not intended to discuss the question, whether or not conviction should take place upon circumstantial evidence alone: all that is meant is to lay down the principle, that the existence of doubt is a ground for acquittal, not for the infliction of a moderated punishment. The Mahometan assessors doubt, yet they strike—with some shew of moderation, indeed, but (according to their own belief) in the dark, as to whether the blow is merited or not. They will not do a great wrong; but they feel no reluctance to inflict a small one.* This specimen is not calculated to impress us with a very high reverence for Mahometan morality and jurisprudence.

The rules which in the Mahometan code govern the reception or rejection of evidence, are remarkably capricious. In capital cases, the testimony of slaves is inadmissible, and some arguments might be brought forward to shew the reasonableness of the disqualification; but the Mahometan law

* Two men were playing at cards, and one of them, who suspected he was cheated, seized a fork, and with it pinned his antagonist's hand to the table, saying, "Sir, if you have not the knave of trumps under your hand, I beg your pardon." This is something like the conduct of the Mahometan lawyers; except in the politeness with which the random punishment was inflicted.

law does not reject the evidence of slaves because it is likely to be unduly influenced by fear, but because "their state of bondage precludes them from exercising any act of authority, which the delivery of evidence is considered to be." The exclusion of slaves, therefore, is not the dictate of legislative prudence, but a mere point of taste and etiquette. The testimony of women is rejected: and as reason can say nothing in favour of such a rule, tradition steps in and pleads the example of the prophet and of his two immediate successors. In minor cases, the testimony of women may be received, but the evidence of two women is only equivalent to that of one man. If the accused person is a Mussulman, the witnesses against him must be of the same faith. The testimony of infidel subjects, with regard to each other, is admissible, whatever variety of belief they may profess; it is also good against an infidel stranger; but the evidence of the latter is invalid, except against one of his own countrymen. Persons of infamous character are not improperly disqualified as witnesses, and certain very close relations, either of consanguinity or social position, constitute grounds of incompetency. The absurdity of many of these exceptions to testimony is obvious, and their inconvenience is equal to their absurdity. The British Government has, however, shewn towards them a tenderness that is remarkable, considering

sidering that the Mahometan faith is not professed by more than an eighth part of the people. Such rules could not be endured, but they have not been directly abrogated. It has been provided, that if the evidence of a witness shall be declared inadmissible on any ground which shall appear unreasonable, the judge shall nevertheless take the examination of the witness. At the conclusion of the trial the Mahometan law officer shall state what would have been the sentence if such evidence had been admissible, and the judge is to pass sentence accordingly; but if the conviction is found to rest exclusively on the excepted evidence, the case is to be referred to the superior tribunal. It is not easy to see the advantages of this circuitous method of getting rid of the consequences of inconvenient and absurd rules of evidence.

The Mahometan law prefers confessions to all other evidence, and the native police neglect no means of obtaining that which the law regards as so desirable. Under the Mahometan government, torture was resorted to for this good end. The British Government, of course, does not countenance such a practice, but frequent instances of its use have come before the tribunals. Some of the tortures employed are too horrible and revolting to be described. It has been found extremely difficult to suppress these practices, the native officers

officers having such an appetite for confessions, that even where the most ample proof exists, they will endeavour to extort them. The judges endeavour to correct the evil, as far as possible, by receiving these confessions with great caution. In Madras, they were formerly required to be attested by two witnesses totally unconnected with the police; but the native officers, whose aptitude for mischief appears to be altogether marvellous, contrived to select, as witnesses, those individuals to whom the duty was peculiarly inconvenient. Some of those persons, in order to avoid being called upon again, had recourse to the ready expedient of perjury, and swore, with great coolness, that they knew nothing about the confessions which were given in their presence. The original rule was then rescinded, and all police officers above the rank of a common peon were admitted as competent witnesses. The consequences of this may readily be conceived.

In speaking of the existing state of law and police in India, we speak of merely temporary arrangements—of a system doomed, at no very distant period, to yield to another. The late Act, after recognizing the expediency of a general system of judicial establishments and police throughout the entire country, directs the appointment of a commission, to inquire into the jurisdiction, power, and rules of the existing courts of justice and

and police establishments; into all existing forms of judicial procedure; and into the nature and operation of all laws, civil or criminal, written or customary, prevailing in any part of the country, and affecting any class of inhabitants, European or native. The results of these inquiries are to be embodied in reports, in which the commissioners are to suggest such alterations and improvements as they shall deem advisable. The Governor General in Council may give special instructions as to the inquiries to be made and the places to be visited, which the commissioners are to regard, and to make special reports upon such matters as may be required. The commission issues from the Governor General in Council, and the members are recommended by the Court of Directors, with the approbation of the Board of Commissioners. Such other persons may be included as the Governor General in Council shall think fit, provided the entire number does not exceed five. The commissioners are to receive salaries, according to the highest scale of remuneration given to any of the officers or servants of the Company, below the rank of members of council.

Viewed in connexion with the appointment of the fourth member of council at the seat of government, this provision is a most important one. The British Legislature evidently contemplated the complete recasting of the institutions of India.

A measure

A measure affecting the interests of so many millions of people, possesses an importance before which all ordinary legislation sinks into insignificance. From the days of Justinian, no labour so difficult, or fraught with such important consequences, has been undertaken; and whether, like the volume of Roman jurisprudence, it shall be destined to descend to the end of time, a monument of legislative genius and sagacity; or, like some less fortunate codes of modern creation, disappear within a brief period after its promulgation, must depend on the character of those to whom its execution is committed. The project is a grand one, whatever its success.

As the task allotted to the law commissioners is by no means easy, the qualifications required for its performance are not few. A comprehensive and accurate knowledge of human nature; an acquaintance with the principal codes of law which have prevailed in the world, and with the manner in which they have operated; a familiarity with the writings of the ablest jurists, and with the principles of moral evidence; an intimacy with the local peculiarities, usages, and modes of thought of the people whom their labours are intended to benefit; strong logical faculties, matured by habitual exercise; great industry and great caution; these are some of the qualifications which are indispensable. All of them can scarcely be be expected in an individual, but by a judicious selection the whole may be secured within the number prescribed by the Act. A perfect freedom from prejudices of every kind will be essential to a due discharge of the duty required of the commissioners, especially from such a prejudice in favour of preconceived theories, as prevents even ingenious and strong-minded men from seeing more than half of any question; and from two prejudices which divide between them the mass of mankind—the prejudice in favour of every thing that exists, and the opposite, equally foolish and perhaps more mischievous prejudice, in favour of every thing that is untried. Possessed of all these qualifications, the framers of a code of law for India must not be in too much haste. Every thing that is important requires to be matured by the operation of time; and legislation is one of the most important works to which the human mind can apply its powers.

In the performance of this work, care must be taken to avoid the error formerly committed, of entrusting too much to native intelligence and discretion. The lawgivers which India has been accustomed to revere have no claim to our favourable consideration, except that which they derive from their influence over the conduct and opinions of so many millions of people. This, however, is not to be disregarded; and we must beware of

 attempting

attempting too hastily to assail any principles which are interwoven with the habits of the people, even though it might appear to us that we could substitute better. We are now, it might be hoped, in little danger of entertaining a blind admiration for the barbarous oracles of Hindoo and Mussulman law; we are, perhaps, more likely to err on the other side, by regarding our own views of what is right or what is expedient, as adapted for universal application, and thus to be induced to force upon India a system of law which she is not prepared to receive, and which is but ill calculated to work for her benefit. We shall commit an error of this kind, if we assume that the natural rights of mankind cannot lawfully receive any modification from natural and local circumstances. Natural rights ought to be respected; but it must be shewn, that the persons on whose behalf they are claimed are in a condition to exercise them, before they can be prudently conceded. The infant, the idiot, and the lunatic, are subjected to restraint. This restraint is not imposed from the love of tyranny, but for the good of the persons over whom it is exercised; and multitudes may sometimes be in a condition, where to entrust them with all which wild, but mistaken philanthropy would claim for them, would be to involve them in certain ruin, and suspend for ages their progress in improvement.

improvement. With India we must probably be content to follow the example of the Grecian legislator, who affirmed that he had given his countrymen not the best laws that could be framed, but the best that they could bear. We must be careful also not to mistake for natural rights those which are not such. We constantly hear the institutions of society condemned, for violating natural rights in cases where nature certainly has given no rule. For instance, the law of primogeniture is frequently declared to be a violation of the law of nature. It would be extremely difficult, however, to show that nature has given any law on the subject; and if she had, it might be presumed that that which has prevailed most generally would be the true one. It is not meant here to offer any opinion on the advantages or disadvantages of the law of primogeniture, but only to contend, that in this and a multiplicity of other cases, where nature has been supposed to speak, she is in truth silent, and has left the matter in question to the decision of human prudence.

But we must guard in the next place against an error of a different kind. A very active and ingenious body of legislators in our own day deny that man has any natural rights at all. They would decide every thing upon the principle of expediency. They estimate the human feelings at nothing. They even despise the intuitive judgments of the human reason, and would dismiss every principle of morals and of legislation which does not present itself as a deduction of the understanding. Like most philosophic exclusives, these legislators are inconsistent with themselves. They assume a single principle, that all legislation should be designed to promote "the greatest happiness of the greatest number." The principle is both absurd and dangerous. If it be just, then, in a country where seven-twelfths of the people had one interest, and the remaining five-twelfths another, the governing powers should legislate for the benefit of the former, regardless of the latter. The absurdity becomes more apparent when the sacrifice is of five to seven; but the hardship and cruelty would be just the same if the numbers were ninety-nine to one. But the principle assumed as the basis of utilitarian legislation, is not only mischievous, but it is inconsistent with the avowed design of its defenders. They will leave nothing to feeling or intuition. The understanding is to be supreme, and no man is to maintain any thing which he cannot support by a formal argument. The sense of justice, the feeling of benevolence, are rejected as insufficient guides. All moral principles must be squared to the rules of expediency. The question, Why must I do what is just? would by most men be

thought

thought an unreasonable one, since in morals, as in every other branch of human enquiry, there must be an ultimate point, beyond which we cannot proceed. But to the expounders of the philosophy of utility, the question would not appear a strange one: they would answer, because, by observing the rules of justice you will promote the greatest happiness of the greatest number. But, surely, the enquirer is not bound to stop here, any more than at the former point. He may demand, why am I bound to promote the greatest happiness of the greatest number? To this the advocate of utility would, probably, answer, by an appeal to the selfish feelings; because, by doing so, you will stand the best chance of promoting your own happiness. But the objector might still demur: he might say, instances continually occur in which I may promote my own benefit by violating those rules which, you say, are essential to the good of the community: why should I not avail myself of such opportunities, and despise those laws which you admit have no better foundation than that of general expediency? You have removed all other sanctions, why should I be stopped by this? To such interrogatories but one answer could be given—the majority have the physical power, and they will compel you to obey the laws of the community, or punish you for your disobedience; and thus the

the reasoner will leap at once from the theory of Priestley and Bentham to that of Hobbes. It is clear, then, that what is called "the greatest happiness principle," so far from being able to support the entire fabric of law and morals, is unable to support itself; so far from being able to give a tone to the moral feelings of the community, it cannot exist but through the influence of moral feelings derived from some other source. The great distinctions of right and wrong exist independently of any calculation of consequences; and happy it is that they do so, for human prudence would afford but a sorry substitute. The mistakes of the wisest and best-intentioned, prove the incompetency of the understanding of man to decide on the best means of promoting his own happiness, or that of his species.

The work of legislation will never be properly performed, if any single principle is assumed as its basis. There must be a compromise among various principles, or the system will never work harmoniously.

The principle of attachment to ancient institutions is one which is powerfully operative among every people, except under very peculiar circumstances. Men yield obedience more readily to that which is old than to that which is new. Innovation is always attended with some danger: and it is not only dangerous to shock the

the feelings of men with regard to that which has the sanction of time and custom, but the experiment when made is seldom successful. Laws and institutions, transplanted from one country to another, rarely work smoothly or beneficially. The *cessio bonorum* of Scotland is not attended by the rich crop of vices which have arisen round the insolvent system of England. The United States of America afford the only instance in modern times, where laws which had grown out of the circumstances of one country have been successfully applied to the government of another. But in this case the people, as well as the laws, derive their origin from the English, and carried with them across the Atlantic a large portion of English thought, feelings, and manners. In India, inhabited as it is by different races of people, it is not necessary, and it will not be prudent, to enforce, in all particulars, a perfect uniformity of law. The law of inheritance is one which must be treated with much forbearance. The Hindoo has one law, the Mahometan another, the Englishman a third, and these may all be recognised, and each party protected in that principle of succession which he possibly deems important. There are other points in which compliance with customs, and even with prejudices when they are harmless, may be necessary. The evils of a contrary practice have been too often exemplified, but

but never more strikingly than by the fate of Joseph of Germany, who, by violent and ill judged attempts to enforce what he believed to be necessary reforms, and to establish uniform institutions throughout his dominions, defeated his own purposes, kindled the flame of rebellion among those whose principle was implicit obedience, and died despairing and broken-hearted, the victim of his own precipitation and obstinacy.

There may, however, be practices so obviously wrong and extensively mischievous, as to merit no toleration. These must be dealt with on other principles. Antiquity and prescription must not be allowed to violate the common rights of mankind. Practices which outrage the great principles of justice and benevolence must be retrenched with an unsparing hand. Man is endowed by his Creator with certain rights, and no government can be justified in permitting these to be invaded with impunity. Oppression must not be supported because it has prevailed from time immemorial. The innocent and the weak must be protected from wrong, though that wrong be offered under the sanction of antiquity, and even enforced by superstition. Government have already acted upon these principles, and they will not go back.

The principle of utility, though it has been abused, must not be altogether rejected. Utility is is an insufficient basis for moral science; but it affords a very good test of the quality of both private and public acts. A law which produces more misery than it prevents is clearly a bad one. In many cases the path of the legislator is not marked out by that higher species of law which he, in common with all mankind, is bound to reverence. Thus left to himself, he must look to probable consequences, and deducing a rule where otherwise he would be left without one, he must, to the best of his ability, strike a balance of good and evil, and preserve as much as may be of the former, with the smallest possible alloy of the latter. The deductions of human prudence are, indeed, but too often fallacious; but in the absence of any other guide it cannot be dispensed with.

The promotion of peace should be an important object with every legislator. This principle is, in some degree, connected with the first and the last, already adverted to; but it is of sufficient importance to merit distinct mention. Peace is an important instrument for securing to society much of good that cannot be obtained without it. But the legislator should not view it merely as an instrument: he should regard it as an end; and in all the institutions which he is called upon to frame, should keep its promotion steadily in view. Its preservation is one of the great purposes for which civil society exists.

The

The principles enumerated may receive some illustration from a subject already mentioned—the inheritance of property. The peace of society requires that some rule should be laid down; the law of nature (the second principle) gives none. The legislator must, therefore, frame one as well as he can with reference to other principles. Utility suggests the adoption of that which is best calculated to promote the prosperity of the community. The law of primogeniture tends to promote the accumulation—that of equal division, the dispersion of wealth. In England, real property descends according to one rule, personal property according to the other; and perhaps this is as beneficial an arrangement as could be adopted, tending, as it does, to check undue accumulation on the one hand, and minute subdivision on the other. But it is a matter of merely prudential arrangement, and circumstances may render it expedient, in some countries, to adopt a different course. India may be one of them. Custom has there laid down different rules for different classes of people, and there may be no sufficient reason for departing from them, especially as their preservation will, in all probability, tend to the preservation of peace. This is a case for the exercise of the discretion of the legislator; but where any great moral law interposes a sanction or a prohibition, he has no option. He cannot change the eternal

eternal distinctions of right and wrong, and he must not legislate in disregard of them.

But he is thus bound only as to the principles of his laws. Justice must be upheld, but by what means must be left to the sagacity of the legislator. The principle of right interferes not with those provisions which regulate the administration of the laws; and those are the best which will promote the ends of justice most completely, and with the least amount of attendant inconvenience. Some regard must, however, generally be paid to existing systems. Where a people have been long accustomed to one mode of administering justice, they will generally look with some distrust upon any other. This, however, scarcely applies at all to India. All the existing courts have been introduced by the English, and consequently within a very short period of time. Even within that period they have been subjected to various changes, and consequently the people cannot be supposed to have formed any very deep-rooted attachment to them. They prefer English courts to those with which they were cursed under their native princes, because the latter were as inefficient for good and as potent for evil as was possible; but their confidence is in the integrity of their rulers, and would readily be given to courts differently modified, if sanctioned by the same authority, and made equally or more beneficial in their operation. As far,

far, therefore, as the arbitrary arrangements for the administration of justice are concerned, the legislator will have little prejudice to contend with. He should therefore strike boldly at the root of existing evils, and not shrink from a measure of sweeping change, if it be called for by the state of the country. In every age, however, there are some prevailing opinions which pass current upon the mere strength of clamour, and which the enlightened legislator must carefully examine previous to adoption. In our own day, there are some errors afloat on the subject of the administration of the law, which like most popular errors are mixed with a small portion of truth, from which they derive their plausibility and currency. There are two assertions which are constantly repeated by a certain class of reasoners, or non-reasoners, with such a degree of confidence as if they were self-evident truths, and at the same time with such an assumption of sagacity as if they were new discoveries. These are, that the administration of justice should be cheap, and that it should be speedy. These assertions cannot be met by a flat denial; but a little examination will shew, that in the unqualified manner in which they are advanced, they are calculated to lead to consequences rather mischievous than beneficial. The promise of cheap justice is very tempting; but then we ought to be sure that the promise will be fulfilled.

fulfilled. If instead of cheap justice we only get cheap law, we shall have small occasion to rejoice. If disputes could be decided without any expense, it might be well: but lawyers will not take the trouble of studying the law for the mere pleasure of administering it; and having studied it, they will not give their time and labour, either in deciding causes or in preparing them for decision, without remuneration. The amount of remuneration will, in a great measure, determine the amount of talent, information, and even of integrity, that shall be brought to the task. If higher emoluments can be commanded by talent in any other profession, talent will not find its way into the law; and no man will consume his days and nights in the acquisition of legal knowledge, if his reward is to be altogether inadequate to his labour. Integrity, it was observed by one of the witnesses before the Parliamentary Committee, is, in some sense, "a purchaseable article." He is most likely to preserve it who is removed from temptation. If a judge or a legal practitioner be but indifferently paid, he may think it not worth while to keep a conscience: but when his emoluments are large, and their continuance dependent upon his good conduct, his interest and his duty draw the same way. To place the judge above temptation, and even above suspicion, is indispensable. But this will not be sufficient, unless

unless the advocates and agents who are required in the conduct of suits are sufficiently rewarded. We see in our own country, that the higher class of attornies are the more respectable, not only in point of circumstances, but in point of character. The lower part of the profession are at once a disgrace and a scourge to the country. In India it appears to be the same. The vakeels in the superior courts are respectable; in the inferior they are not. As a general rule, to keep men respectable, you must keep them above want; you may pay judges at a cheap rate, but their quality will be proportioned to their price; and stupid, ignorant, and corrupt judges are always dear enough. Under no system of law can professional advice and assistance be altogether dispensed with. You may have that, too, at any price; but if you would secure ability, knowledge, industry, and faithfulness, you must offer such terms as will command these qualities. The course of justice, then, cannot be very cheap: the charges necessary to secure its purity must ever prevent its being so. If law be rendered very cheap, it will be inefficient and corrupt. Instead of affording protection, it will become an instrument of oppression and wrong. Much has been said of the advantages of placing law within the reach of the poor. For the most part, they are much happier in keeping out of it; and it seems to be forgotten, that where the parties

ties are in different circumstances, the rich man is generally the plaintiff and the poor man the defendant. The former is sometimes deterred from proceeding by the apprehension that he may gain nothing but a bill of costs. Take away this fear, and actions will be multiplied to an enormous extent. Is it necessary, in India, to stimulate the litigious propensities of the natives?

The other demand, that justice should not only be cheap but speedy, must, like its fellow, not be conceded without some considerable qualification. There must be sufficient time for bringing the case properly before the court; sufficient time for hearing it calmly and deliberately, and sufficient time for weighing and considering its merits; and afterwards, if the parties are dissatisfied, sufficient time for consideration on appeal, or, if necessary, for a new trial. Complaints of the law's delay are so ancient and universal, that we may almost conclude that a considerable portion of delay is inevitable. Even this, like the expense of law, is not without its counterbalancing advantages. It affords time for accommodation, and disposes men to accede to it. If this be not enough to justify, it is something to extenuate the evil of delay. In many cases, time will enable a defendant to meet the claim of his creditor which he could not satisfy if pressed at once. Men frequently say one thing whilst they intend another; and when creditors

creditors cry out for speedy justice, they mean speedy judgment and execution.

The question of the employment of natives in judicial situations occupied a considerable share of the attention of the late Parliamentary Committee. It is attended with considerable difficulties. The notorious want of moral principle in the natives generally, is a formidable objection to their employment in judicial services beyond all others, while the impossibility of providing a sufficient number of Europeans to perform them, scarcely leaves a choice on the subject. The question has been settled, in point of fact, by the extensive jurisdiction which has been bestowed upon the native judges. This having taken place, there is no going back. Whatever courts may be established, and whatever the modes of practice, the judicial functions must be exercised to a great extent by natives. No people should be regarded as unimprovable, and it may be hoped, that a better state of moral feeling may in time prevail in India. In the mean while, all that can be done to secure the integrity of the native judges must be attended to. They ought to be remunerated, not only fairly but liberally. None should be appointed but men respectable in point of character as well as of talent and attainments, and their proceedings should be subjected to the vigilant superintendence of Europeans. It has been

been suggested, that it might be desirable to bestow upon them pensions, after a certain period of service. Perhaps this might be made an instrument of securing their good conduct. The salary might be a moderate one, but the pension on retirement considerable: the latter to be entirely forfeited in case of misconduct. In the event of the death of a judge before the period allowed for retirement, a sum proportioned to his length of service might be paid to his heirs, subject to the same conditions as those of the pension. It is certain that it will at present not be easy to secure the purity of native judges, and whatever promises to promote this end deserves consideration. It has been assumed by many, that the way to raise the character of the natives will be, to treat them with confidence. This conclusion seems to be scarcely warranted by experience. Undoubtedly, one of the most effectual modes of weakening the principles of an honest and honourable man, is to treat him with unjust suspicion. He becomes degraded in his own estimation, in proportion as he perceives himself to have fallen in that of others, and one powerful restraint upon his conduct is removed. But, though the withholding confidence may impair the character of an honest man, it may be doubted whether the bestowal of confidence will raise the character of a dishonest one. At all events, the experiment is a hazardous one. Confidence, too, though it may be dissembled in such a case, cannot be felt. It is, as Lord Chatham observed, "a plant of slow growth;" and when, for a succession of years, nothing has appeared but deception and chicane, credulity itself cannot believe that sincerity and straightforwardness should arise at a moment's notice. Confidence, however, or the appearance of it, has been yielded. The step has been taken, and cannot be recalled. But we must not be too sanguine in the belief, that our confidence will not be in many cases abused.

In placing the law of India on a permanent footing, the conflicting jurisdictions of the King's and the Company's courts must be accommodated. The Supreme Court appears to be, in many respects, ill adapted for the country, and some of its modes of procedure to be ill adapted to promote the ends of justice in any country. That a man who has reason to believe himself out of the jurisdiction of the court, should be liable to be arrested, and carried several hundred miles, to answer in an action which may turn out to be frivolous, or even groundless, is a grievance which ought not to continue for a single month. The aversion of the natives to the Supreme Court has, probably, as much of prejudice as of rational objection; but there is certainly enough in some of its proceedings to justify the feeling. The Supreme

Court

Court ought not to be permitted, and in all probability will not be permitted, to exist according to its present practice and constitution. It might, perhaps, be incorporated with the general system of the courts of the country in such a way as to become a useful appendage to them. What that system will be must at present be vain to anticipate.

The first thing necessary will be to provide sufficient courts of primary jurisdiction. Under the system hitherto prevailing in India, there have been courts of different grades, rising above one another in the amount on which they could adjudicate. This system is radically vicious, and its evil tendency is forcibly exposed by Mr. Mill. He says: "Another objection of mine to the courts of India is, that they have been established upon the principle of one sort of courts for sums of small amount, another sort for sums of higher—the best tribunals for the highest sums, the worst tribunals for the lowest; declaring, in fact, that more care is due to prevent wrongs done to the rich than wrongs done to the poor." This is an error into which legislators are very apt to fall. The sum in dispute is small, and they refer it to an inferior judge; but the difficulty of adjudicating properly with regard to a small sum, may be as great as with regard to a large one. A claim for 100 rupees may be beset

 with

with many difficulties, both as to law and fact; a claim for 10,000 may be very plain with regard to both. It is obviously unreasonable to assign the difficult and complicated case to the inferior judge, merely because it involves only a small sum, and the plain case to a more competent judge, because the sum claimed is a large one; and it is not less invidious than unreasonable. All causes, whatever be the value of the matter in dispute, should come before the same judge. The sum in question may be a trifle: but justice is not a trifle, and justice should be dispensed to the poor man as well as to the rich.

All petty courts should be forthwith abolished, and respectable judges, with adequate pecuniary advantages, appointed to preside in the courts of primary jurisdiction. To secure impartiality, no judge should be fixed in any particular district. A local judge never can be impartial. Even if his intentions are good, he in many cases must become a partizan, in spite of himself. By long residence, he becomes intimately acquainted with many of the persons who must appear before him, either as parties to suits or witnesses. If the district be neither large nor populous, he will in no great length of time be acquainted almost with every person in it, and it will be impossible to keep his mind free from prepossessions and prejudices. If the judges must be local, they should

be

be removed from one district to another at intervals. But it would be much better that a plan should be adopted somewhat similar to the English circuits. A number of judges might be assigned to a given division of the country, which should be subdivided into a number of circuits. At stated and convenient periods the judges should visit the circuits, to administer justice, care being taken that no individual judge went the same circuit too frequently. The courts should be opened at various places, so as to diminish, as much as possible, the distance which parties and witnesses would have to travel, and thus to cut off one important source of expense. It is absolutely necessary to the pure administration of justice, that the judges, of the primary courts should be ambulatory. Even in our own country, where the means of publicity are so great, and the checks on the bench so numerous, the system of Welsh judicature was, on account of its localization, found to be fraught with such a mass of abuse, as to call for its abolition by the Legislature.

In each division there might be a judge of appeal, who should always be a European. Mr. Mill's view of the functions of an appellate judge appears to be the correct one. He should, in no case, hear new evidence, which is, in fact, to retry the cause. Upon the view of the pleadings and evidence, he should either confirm, vary, or

reverse

reverse the decree of the court below; or if he think that evidence has been improperly rejected, he should send back the case for a fresh hearing.

Further, there might be one superior court of appeal for the whole of the British possessions in India. Mr. Mill has shewn the importance of such a court, in securing uniformity in the law, and the advantages which would result from placing it at Calcutta. But he would do away with intermediate appeals, and in this point the soundness of his views is open to doubt. If all appeals went at once to the highest court, the judges must be very numerous, or the court would be overloaded with business. By interposing the first appeal, this inconvenience would be avoided. Many cases would stop there, and the judges of the highest court would have sufficient time to give proper attention to those that came before them. Mr. Mill's opinion, that one judge is preferable to a plurality, will probably not find many supporters. The judges should sit together in number not less than three. Mr. Mill alleges, that the time which they would consume in talking of the case would be saved if only a single judge sate. This may be true; but it is surely important, and more especially so in a tribunal of the last resort, that causes should receive due consideration. It is more important that they should be decided justly, than that they should be decided

cided quickly. Possibly the supreme courts might be incorporated with the high court of appeal; but, however constituted, the judgments of this court should be final. The appeal to England should be abolished. There can be no reason to doubt that justice can be secured in India; and if so, why should either persons or papers traverse half the world in search of that which may be had at home?

It has been proposed to give the European judges a concurrent jurisdiction with the native judges. It would surely be better to confine their attention to appeals and applications for new trials. If it be desirable to endeavour to raise the character of the native judges, they ought not to be brought into immediate comparison with Europeans. The time of the European judges, too, would, in all probability, be sufficiently occupied by appeals.

The proper mode of paying the judges gives rise to a question of some importance, but regarding which there is little ground for difference of opinion. They should receive adequate salaries, and neither depend wholly or in part upon fees. Where a judge is paid by fees, there is a door opened to abuses of the worst description. Among other results, the decision of such a judge is always in favour of the plaintiff, if he can find a decent pretext for it. It may be true, that he may get no more in one case than in the other; but he

indirectly

indirectly promotes his interests by tempting suitors into his court.

The modes of procedure before the Court of Primary Jurisdiction cannot be expected to vary much from those which are now in use. The pleadings appear to be reduced to as much simplicity as they are capable of; and if they are frequently defective, in consequence of being prepared by ignorant persons, the only proper remedy is to provide for the people a better set of legal advisers. The practice of oral pleading would throw great power into the hands of the judge; and with native judges, especially, this is not expedient. The privilege which it has been proposed to concede to the judge, of determining what witnesses should be called, would enable him to give any judgment he pleased, and preserve at the same time an appearance of decency. To avoid the existing evil, and the still greater evil which would result from the proposed remedy, the courts of India must be assisted by respectable legal practitioners, competent to the duties required of them. Whether they should unite the two characters of attorney and advocate, or whether these two classes should be kept distinct, may be best determined on the spot. Their fees should be regulated, and they should certainly not be paid as the vakeels at present are, by a per-centage on the amount in dispute. It will

be

be important to render them amenable for their conduct, and at the same time to free them from slavish dependence upon the native judge. With this view, they should be removable only by the Judge of Appeal. Due provision should be made for the admission of none but men of competent knowledge in the law, and of respectable character. As nothing tends more to promote litigation, and its consequent misery, than a herd of unprincipled and starving lawyers, it might be desirable to limit the number of these officers. There should be no more than are likely to obtain a livelihood; at the same time they should be sufficiently numerous for the transaction of business without confusion or delay, to ensure the advantages of competition, and to give the client a reasonable choice.

The administration of the criminal law might be placed in the same hands as that of the civil law. There seem no good reasons for dividing, and there are some for uniting them under one jurisdiction. The European judges should, however, keep a vigilant eye upon the conduct of the natives, in the exercise of their criminal, as well as their civil authority, and the punishment of death should never be inflicted except with the sanction of the highest court. The gaol deliveries should be frequent. In civil matters, a slight delay is of small importance; but to subject an innocent

cent man to unnecessary imprisonment is a serious evil. As the judges would not, like those of England, be required to sit *in banco,* they might be almost constantly upon circuit, and the time between committal and trial need in no case be a long one.

Englishmen are naturally attached to the mode of trial by jury, and their attachment is natural and just. Trial by jury is, perhaps, the best protection which human sagacity ever devised against that worst species of tyranny which invades the rights of mankind, under the mask of law. Its indirect effects in maintaining the love of justice and freedom among a people, and in diffusing a pure and elevated public spirit, are scarcely less beneficial; and with these views, from which few Englishmen will dissent, we must be desirous to see trial by jury extended to every part of the dominions subjected to British sway. It has been proposed to extend it to India; but is India prepared to receive and benefit by it? There is, as has been observed, "a great want of the materials necessary to compose tribunals at all resembling English juries." It is admitted, that there will be some difficulty in finding a sufficient number of natives qualified in point of integrity to undertake the judicial office. Can there, in such a society, be any hope of getting an honest and impartial jury? In striking a jury, no great selection

tion can be used. It must be made up from a certain class taken almost indiscriminately. Trial by jury is an admirable institution; but it supposes a high tone of moral sentiment diffused among the people, and, admirable as it is, it has scarcely answered any where as an instrument of justice, except in Great Britain and the United States of America. In France, it is a decided failure. In India, besides being inexpedient, it would be highly unpopular. Where men are totally absorbed in self, they will feel annoyed at being called from the care of their own business to attend to that of others without reward; this would be felt as a grievance, and they would, no doubt, endeavour to remedy it by selling themselves to the party best able to purchase. The power entrusted to native judges will require to be carefully guarded. But it is possible to give a judge, who is a paid officer, a direct interest in doing right. A jury must, in a great degree, be irresponsible, and the Hindoos are not in a condition to be trusted with irresponsible power.

An institution bearing some resemblance, though a distant one, to a jury, has long existed among the Hindoos under the name of a punchayet. This is a body composed of private individuals, originally five, but now varying in number, to whom disputes are referred by the consent of the parties, and in some cases the Company's courts have

have availed themselves of its use. The natives have no partiality for officiating on these tribunals. They are not willing, said the Bengal Government in 1827, "to sacrifice their time without remuneration, for the benefit of their neighbours or for the public good. They know that their award will, in all human probability, make one of the parties their enemy; and they are too well aware of the character of their countrymen, to doubt that the first mark of such enmity would generally be an accusation, whether just or unfounded, that they had given such award under the influence of partiality or corruption." Considerable solicitation is generally necessary to overcome this reluctance, and this is not unfrequently enforced by the more powerful advocacy of presents. The proceedings of punchayets are, as might be expected, exceedingly disorderly, and their decisions give little satisfaction. They are either distinguished by gross negligence, or if any interest is excited, it is of an improper character, arising from the fact of each individual member regarding himself, not as a judge to decide according to truth and equity, but as an advocate who is to do the best for the person who has retained him. Their conduct as jurors would, doubtless, be similar. They would either let the judge think for them, in which case their attendance would be useless, or each man would fight for

for his particular client, which would be mischievous. When India is qualified to appreciate the invaluable blessing of trial by jury, and to use it well and wisely, it ought to be conceded; till then, it is charity as well as wisdom to withhold it. Whenever the period of introducing it may arrive, it should be upon the English principle of requiring unanimity in the verdict. This is a security against corruption, because it is more easy to corrupt a part than the whole; it is a security for full examination, because difference of opinion, if it exist, cannot be removed without discussion; it is, in a certain degree, a security for a just decision, because, in the interchange of opinion imposed by the necessity of discussion, the influence of discrimination and integrity will be considerable. Trial by jury, where unanimity is not required, deserves not the name. In no country is the institution thus deprived of one of its limbs of any value. In India especially, the decision of a mere majority of jurors could command no respect, and the verdict might almost as well be made to depend upon the toss of a rupee.

The language in which a large portion of the proceedings of the courts in India are transacted is the Persian—not the language of the country, but introduced by those who subjugated it. It is a language, however, very generally studied and understood by the educated classes, and on this account,

account, probably, has hitherto deserved the preference which has been given it. If superseded, as it perhaps ultimately will be by the English, the process must be very gradual. Until the latter language is as well understood as the former, great inconveniences would arise from its introduction, causing, among others, the exclusion of native pleaders from practice. For many reasons we must be desirous of extending the use of our native tongue; but this, like many other good ends, must not be urged with too much precipitancy.

To lay down scientific and just rules of evidence for the guidance of the courts, and to frame a system of conveyancing adapted to the country, will be two important and most useful labours. The former will be a comparatively simple task, as there is little reason for varying the rules of evidence in any country. In criminal proceedings, the interrogation of accused persons, and other odious practices, sanctioned by the codes of some countries, though happily not by the law of England, should be carefully avoided, and the wise and humane maxims which among us have passed into axioms, that "every man should be presumed to be innocent until he is proved guilty," and that "it is better that ten guilty persons should escape than that one innocent man should suffer," should be steadily kept in view. In civil cases, although the

the disqualifications of witnesses should not be unnecessarily multiplied, the parties to the suits should be rigorously excluded. Their examination would be productive of nothing but abundance of perjury; and in the courts of India it will be unnecessary to offer a bounty on the fabrication of false testimony. The supply will be quite sufficient without it.

To frame a judicious system of conveyancing will be a work of greater difficulty, and will require a most intimate and minute acquaintance with the nature of Indian tenures, so widely differing from those of Europe, and of our own country espcially. In matters of evidence, an English lawyer of enlarged mind and knowledge would be the best guide; in conveyancing, he would probably be the worst. The subject must be approached with extreme caution, and information must be sought with the most sedulous care; for it is a fact, that notwithstanding a large part of India has been so long subject to our rule, we are yet but imperfectly acquainted with the nature and conditions of landed tenures in that country. A system of registration will, in all probability, form part of the new law. In some countries—in our own, for instance—the advantages of such a plan are very doubtful, and a large portion of the community regard its evils as greater than its benefits. But where fraud is of such constant occurrence

rence as in India, there will be little security for property without it. The attendant evil will not be so great as in a nation of higher feeling and greater refinement; but whether great or small, it is one which, under the present circumstances, must be submitted to, in order to avoid something worse.

CHAPTER XI.

REVENUE.

In India, the great source from which the financial wants of the state are supplied is the land revenue. The modes of its collection and administration are various. One of these modes is distinguished by the name of the zemindary system. Under this system may be classed all those cases in which any portion of land beyond that of a village is rated at a certain sum in the gross, and the payment of that sum undertaken by an individual, usually called a zemindar. He, of course, collects from the actual cultivators the sums necessary to make up the amount for which he is accountable. Occasionally the office of zemindar is exercised, not by an individual, but by a small number of persons. In some cases, parties claim the office by hereditary right; in others, it is held only for a term, sometimes a very short one. In extent the variations are not less considerable, ascending from two villages to an entire district, and even a whole province. In the lower provinces of Bengal the zemindary system is universal; all the zemindars are recognized as hereditary, and the amount to be levied upon each is fixed in perpetuity.

The ryotwar system derives its appellation from the class of persons who are immediately subject to it. Ryot is the specific name of the tiller of the soil, and under this system he makes his payment directly to an officer of the Government. The ryotwar system admits of two varieties. According to one, a sum is assessed upon each ryot for the whole of what he cultivates; by the other, which was introduced by Sir Thomas Munro, each field is separately assessed, and the payment of the ryot is made up of the sums specially charged upon the several portions of land which he has in cultivation.

Between the two systems already described stands a third, which has been called the village system. As the name implies, each village under this mode of assessment is rated at an aggregate sum, and an individual is held answerable for the amount. The choice of the person whose duty it is to make up and pay over to the officers of Government the amount of the assessment, is not regulated by any uniform principle. In some cases, particular individuals or families claim a right to the office; in others, the agents are chosen by the village; in others, again, they are selected by the Government.

The Madras presidency is partly under zemindary

dary settlement and partly under a ryotwar assessment. In Bombay all the three systems are in operation.

The importance of the land revenue renders the mode of collection a point of considerable consequence, it being, of course, desirable to transfer the largest amount into the public treasury with the least possible inconvenience to those from whom it is drawn. Some observations will hereafter be made upon the various systems which have been resorted to with this view; but it will be proper previously to advert briefly to the other sources of Indian revenue.

These are the monopolies of salt, opium, and tobacco;—the inland transit duties, originating under native rule, but retained, for the most part, in a modified form, by the British Government;—the customs, under which head are included the duty on saltpetre and the monopoly of cardamums;—a number of minor imposts, sometimes called sayer duties;—the duties included under the term abkaree, comprising those on spirituous liquors, intoxicating drugs, and some other articles;—the town duties, formerly applied to local improvements, but now merged in the general revenue;—the wheel-tax, levied upon hackerys, carts, buggys, &c.;—the post-office, and the stamp-duties.

The monopoly of Salt exists in Madras and the

 lower

lower provinces of Bengal. The Company make advances to a description of persons called Molunghees, who are the manufacturers. In Bengal the salt is disposed of by auction at monthly sales; and the price, on an average of three years, has been found to be about 288 per cent. above the original cost and charges. In Madras the salt is sold at a fixed price, which does not exceed one-fourth of the average price in Bengal; but it is said that the profit derived from it is greater, the cost of production being comparatively small.

Various objections have been taken to this source of revenue, and one of them is certainly not undeserving of consideration. It cannot be denied that a regulation which, for the mere purpose of revenue, adds enormously to the price of an article which must be regarded as a prime necessary of life, is an evil of no small magnitude. But those who urge this are bound to shew how the same amount of revenue could be raised less injuriously. It is quite clear that it must be raised by some means. The wants of the state must be provided for, and an annual deficiency of upwards of a million and a-half sterling, which would result from the abolition of the salt monopoly, could not be supplied with any degree of certainty from new sources. Upon this ground the Company have been permitted, notwithstanding the extinction of their commercial character, to retain this and a

few

few other branches of trade, which they possess exclusively. The objection, grounded on the simple allegation of the generally odious character of monopoly, is unworthy of notice. An enlightened legislature will not be influenced by mere words. It is not enough to say, that this or that branch of revenue is derived from monopoly, to warrant its condemnation. The proper questions are—is the monopoly practically injurious, and will the state of the revenue afford the diminution which will result from its abolition? If the answer to either of these questions be in the negative, the mere term monopoly must not be allowed to have any weight. An excise regulation has been suggested as a substitute; but the expense would be much greater than under the present system, and the protection to the revenue much less. If the same amount were to be raised, the charge to the consumer could not be reduced; and if he were to pay as much in the shape of excise duty as he now pays in another form, it would be difficult to shew how he would be benefited. It has been said that a cheaper supply could be obtained by importation from the coasts of Coromandel and Malabar, Ceylon, the Gulph of Persia, and even Great Britain; but then it must be subjected to a custom-house duty, for the purpose of securing the revenue. If the state can spare the revenue, let the trade be thrown open;

open; if it cannot, the importation must be so regulated as not to interfere in any way with its interests.

The situation of the producers of salt has been represented as very lamentable; but on this point the evidence is in some degree conflicting. Mr. Tucker, a high authority, places them "among the worst-conditioned of our native subjects, from climate, situation, and the nature of their labour." Mr. Holt Mackenzie takes a different view of their condition, which he "believes to be generally better than that of the general cultivators of the country." Between the opinions of two gentlemen, having enjoyed the means of personal observation, it would be arrogant to attempt to decide. If the more gloomy view be the correct one, it may be desirable, on that ground, to discontinue the manufacture of salt, except in the most favourable situations, and to supply the deficiency by importation, due care being taken that the revenue is protected, and also that those persons thrown out of employment should not sustain permanent injury. It deserves notice, also, that some prejudices exist in favour of Bengal salt, though inferior to the produce of other countries. Peculiarity of taste and superstitious feeling combine to sanction these prejudices.

Opium affords another source of revenue which, like salt, is branded with the name of monopoly.

As

As in this case it cannot be pretended that the article monopolized is a necessary of life, or even, generally speaking, conducive to human comfort, justly understood, there is less room for declamatory appeals in favour of freedom, and less to excuse the placing a large amount of revenue in jeopardy for the sake of a political experiment. The monopoly exists throughout the whole of India; but the opium is principally raised in the provinces of Bahar and Benares, which are peculiarly favourable to its cultivation. The Company make advances to the cultivator of the poppy, and when the opium is made, it is delivered into their warehouses; but the Company do not export it. It is disposed of to merchants by public auction; thenceforth the trade is perfectly open, and most of the commercial houses in Calcutta are engaged in it. Very little is consumed in India, and, as has already been intimated, the larger portion finds its way to China. This source of revenue has been considerably affected by the opium introduced from Malwa and other places. To conciliate the natives of central India, the monopoly has been in some degree relaxed, and opium passes through the British territories on payment of transit duties, or by issuing a permit or license in consideration of a certain sum, which enables opium, belonging to the parties who obtain it, to pass without interruption.

Tobacco

Tobacco is, perhaps, a less unobjectionable article of monopoly, which in this case is partial; but as far as it extends its operation appears to be injurious. It places beyond the reach of the larger class of consumers an article which is much desired; and the use of which is said to be beneficial to them under their local circumstances. The protection against smuggling is very inefficient, and great outrages are occasionally committed by those engaged in the illicit trade.

The Post Office is in almost all countries a monopoly. India is an exception to this rule. The present mode of conveying the mail is by runners, who travel at the rate of about four miles an hour. In some parts of the Deccan, a horse post has been tried, and in one instance a light carriage. The nature of the country is at present unfavourable for the use of these improvements; but as it advances in prosperity, the importance of rapid and certain modes of communication will become apparent, and the means will doubtless be provided. The post is yet little used by the natives, and the revenue derived from it is trifling.

Transit Duties form a source of revenue of very old standing in India. They were levied by the native princes, though not precisely under their present system; and even the great zemindars assumed, with or without authority, the power of collecting duties on merchandize passing through their

their zemindaries. This was, of course, productive of great evil and vexation, which the British authority gradually endeavoured to correct. The reform was begun in Bengal, Bahar, and Benares: by Regulations bearing date 1793 and 1795, all internal duties which had been collected by individual landholders and farmers were abolished. In the Ceded and Conquered Provinces, the same plan was followed on their acquisition, and all collections were regulated by specific enactments. But no uniform system was adopted: one method being pursued in the Ceded and Conquered Provinces, another in Benares, and a third in Bengal, Bahar, and Orissa. These various systems continued to prevail until 1810, when a general revision took place, and all those provinces were placed under one law. In Delhi, however, the duties continued to be collected very much according to the native plan, to as late a period as the year 1823, except that they were collected on account of Government. In that year the general system was extended to Delhi. In the territories conquered under the administration of the Marquis of Hastings, the same system has been established with some modifications: in those obtained from the Burmese, it is understood that there are no transit duties. In Madras, the system is uniform, and the old duties have been entirely abolished. In Bombay, the old duties still continue

continue to be levied. In the native states, though the British influence prevails, we, of course, have no direct power to interfere with the internal management of their revenues. With Oude, a commercial treaty concluded by Lord Cornwallis is still considered to be in force. By that treaty the Government of Oude is bound to admit British goods at certain fixed duties, and the British Government not to levy more than two-and-a-half per cent. on the piece-goods of Oude. In some other instances, special agreements have been made with petty chiefs, and compensation given them on condition of their relinquishing the transit duties. But in most of these cases it has subsequently been found desirable to procure the annulment of these agreements, there being good reason to believe that the native princes took the compensation and levied the duties as usual.

The transit duties are generally levied *ad valorem*. The officers by whom these duties are collected are usually natives; and it is suspected that the sums levied upon the trader much exceed the amount which finds its way into the coffers of Government. These duties are, undoubtedly, a great inconvenience and impediment to trade, and it is upon the internal trade of India that they weigh most oppressively; but the amount of the evil cannot be estimated in money. At every stage, goods are liable to examination: and thus, where

where no additional duty is to be levied, additional trouble and vexation are incurred. The trader is placed, in a great degree, at the mercy of a set of rapacious underlings, whose forbearance he will naturally be disposed to purchase with something more than they could lawfully demand. Sometimes, no doubt, the trader and the revenue officer find it convenient to promote their personal interests at the expense of the state. These duties are certainly not productive in any reasonable proportion to the amount of the burden imposed upon the subject. They tend to introduce considerable inequalities in the price of commodities in different parts of the country, and have, in fact, almost every characteristic of vicious taxation. The means of dispensing with them altogether has long occupied the attention of the authorities at home; but unfortunately the amount of revenue cannot be spared, and an eligible substitute is not readily found. An increase of the sea customs has been recommended, but the productiveness of such a measure may be doubted. It is clear, however, that the transit duties form an injurious bar to the commercial advancement of India, and that they should be abolished as early as prudence will admit.

The Customs, a source of revenue to which almost all governments apply, of course partake of the good and the evil which characterize the same mode

mode of taxation in other countries, and will therefore need no particular remark. One or two other branches of revenue are, however, occasionally mixed up with this. Of these, the revenue derived from Saltpetre is rather of the nature of of an excise duty. It is confined to Tirhoot alone, the right in other places having been transferred to the zemindars. The Government claim a share in the produce (said to be a quarter), which is valued in money. Cardamums, in Malabar, are regarded as a royalty. They are an indigenous mountain produce, and it is believed that the only care bestowed in the cultivation is burning the trees around. A farmer takes the farm in the aggregate, paying for it at a certain rate per candy, according to the amount of produce he calculates upon being able to realize. He also pays the mountain proprietor his share of one-half in money at the price at which he farms the produce from Government. The collection is farmed to the highest bidder, to whom the cultivator is bound to deliver his whole produce, and with a view to his protection the Government directs that he shall receive about two-thirds of the market price. This, however, the contractor finds various means of evading; for native ingenuity, when stimulated by avarice, is great. The quantity of cardamums raised is not considerable.

The term "Sayer duties" seems to have been applied

applied with a most convenient latitude of meaning; and any tax which could not readily be referred to any other class, has been placed among the "Sayer duties." Mr. Stark says, that "the term sayer is very often used without meaning any thing more than that the thing spoken of is a duty." If this be correct, the epithet might be dispensed with without much inconvenience. It appears that Lord Cornwallis meant by "sayer duties" the irregular collections made by native officers. When the permanent settlements were made, these duties were abolished, and less exceptionable means of raising a revenue resorted to. In Madras, the transit duties are frequently called sayer duties, when spoken of in the reports of officers; and all collections from inconsiderable sources are in the accounts brought under the general term sayer. In Bengal, the pilgrim tax, when it existed, was included under this head. Colonel Sykes says, that "sayer, in its origin, is a Sanscrit word, meaning market;" that in the Deccan, this source of revenue is divided into two great heads, the first denominated mohturfa, which embraces taxes on shops, trades, &c.; the other ballooteh, which comprehends taxes upon the fees in kind received by the village artizans from the cultivators, and upon their *enam* (rent-free) lands when they hold them. In one instance, the per-centage upon bad coins was found

to

to be included under the head Sayer. This is one of those numerous contrivances by which the ingenuity of native financiers sought to enhance the returns to the treasury without alarming the people by an increased assessment. It is usually called "sherusteh butta, or customary per-centage on the difference between the coin in which the lands were originally assessed, and the coin in which the cultivators paid their taxes." When they paid in inferior coin, such a per-centage was reasonable enough, but when in the current coin it certainly ought not to have been levied. Yet in the village accounts of the Deccan this appears as a permanent charge, although the cultivator pays in the Government rupee; and if he pays in any inferior coin, he has to pay the per-centage upon that particular coin, according to the bazaar rate. Besides this, a number of extra cesses prevail in the Deccan, amounting in the whole to about sixty, and from three to twenty are found in the same village. These are, however, under the authority of Government; but it seems probable that a large part of the amount never reaches its hands, but is diverted to the benefit of district and village officers. "Most of these cesses," says Colonel Sykes, "profess to bear directly on the land: such as those for grain, forage, ropes to Government, dry grain to Ramooses, havildars, gossawees, and the meeras' tax, and tax for sugar. Others,

Others, which originally fell upon trades, such as those for skins, shoes, wool, blankets, oil, &c. &c., are no longer derived from their legitimate sources, but fall upon the cultivator. Other cesses are for milch cattle, fowls, mango-trees, pumpkin-beds, ghee or butter, sour milk, fowls, and fruit; all these extra cesses are called puttees. Some of them involve personal labour, such as those for cutting grass furnished gratis to Government for fire-wood; for dinner-plates, made up of leaves; for monsoon great coats, made of wicker-work and leaves, and for sticks to pound rice with. The rabta mahr is in lieu of personal service. Some of them in their name indicate their temporary character, such as the Eksallee, or for one year; yet they have been continued ever since. There are many others; the shadee puttee, or marriage cess at Angur, amounts to nearly twelve per cent. upon the whole revenue. That could only have been for a passing event, yet it has been continued." These extraordinary imposts are productive of great inconvenience, and easily abused to purposes of oppression. The attention of Government has been called to the subject, and a revenue survey was begun, the object of which was to measure the lands accurately, to assess them according to their productive powers, as far as consistent with individual rights, on which many of these cesses depend and merge,

merge, all that could be abolished in the land tax. It might be well to purchase the rights of individuals, where they stand in the way of improvement. The jastie puttees, a name given to miscellaneous cesses, not falling on the produce of either land or trade, have been abolished throughout all the territories which have been acquired since 1813.

To the duties falling under the term Abkaree, which consist principally of those upon intoxicating liquors and drugs, there can be little objection. They are levied partly by a fixed tax upon the drugs and liquors and partly by a license to retailers. The collections are very minute, and in some instances the licenses stipulate for daily payments.

The Town Duties are levied upon certain articles on their being brought into the cities and chief towns, either for store or consumption. Among the articles are, rice, wheat, barley, ghee, oil, sugar, molasses, tobacco, betel-nut, charcoal, firewood, salt, opium, piece-goods, shawls, rose-water, spirituous liquors, pepper, wax-candles, saltpetre, and spices. But the Regulations vary, and some articles liable to duty under one Government are exempted under another. The amount also varies considerably. In Bengal these duties originally formed part of the general revenue. While Mr. Adam acted as Governor-general,

general, the Government, supposing that it had a surplus revenue, appropriated the town-duties to local purposes, such as improvements in the streets, roads, bridges, and other public works. Since that period, however, this application of the funds derived from the town-duties has ceased, and they have been brought back to their original destination. In Madras, the town-duties are considered as forming part of the sayer, and it does not appear that either there or in Bombay they were ever applied otherwise than to general purposes. These taxes are liable to the same objections as the transit-duties, and where the amount levied is considerable, they must be felt as severe local burdens. They are certainly opposed to all enlightened principles of finance; but the necessity of the state is paramount in its claim, and any measures for their abolition must be taken with a due regard to the security of the revenue.

On the wheel-tax the information to be obtained is very scanty. It seems to be confined to Bombay, and as far as it applies to carts is represented to be injurious and oppressive. The amount derived from it is probably small; and if it be in any degree an impediment, either to agriculture or trade, it may be desirable to abolish it, and to supply the deficiency from some less objectionable source.

Stamp-duties were first imposed in Bengal in 1797,

1797, when legal proceedings were subjected to them. In 1824 the principle of the English law was adopted. Instruments now required to be stamped are contracts, deeds, conveyances, leases, powers of attorney, policies of insurance, bills of exchange, promissory notes, bail bonds, and legal proceedings generally. Bills under twenty-five rupees, and receipts under fifty, are exempted. In Madras the stamp-duties were established in 1808, but were in a great measure confined to legal proceedings. In 1816 they were extended to bonds, bills of exchange, and receipts, as well as to deeds, leases, and mortgages. In Bombay stamp-duties were established in the year 1815.

The question of stamp-duties in India must be decided in a great degree upon general principles. If they are moderate, they appear to be, for the most part, a source of revenue as little exceptionable as most others. With regard to that class which are required on the transfer of property, and on various commercial transactions, the payment of the duty is not without an equivalent, in the increased security afforded to the parties against forgery and fraud; which, by the imposition of stamp-duties, are rendered more difficult of perpetration and more easy of detection. Instances of their utility in this respect might be adduced in our own country. In India, where the danger is much greater, the additional security

security must be proportionately more valuable. An inquiry was instituted by Sir Thomas Munro, while governor of Madras, to ascertain the effect of this class of stamp duties, and the judges reported, that the use of stamped paper had considerably checked the forgery of deeds and other documents. Stamp duties, however, can only be defended when they are of moderate amount. When raised beyond this point, they press severely both on the agricultural and commercial interests, and seriously impede the prosperity of a country.

The stamp duties on law proceedings may be differently judged, according to the light in which they are viewed. On the one hand, they tend to discourage litigation, an important object in India; on the other, their expense may, in some cases, amount to a denial of justice. It is no easy matter to strike a just balance between the good and the evil likely to arise from their retention or abandonment. Perhaps a middle course would be the wisest—to reduce, but not altogether to abolish them. But in the determination of this and all similar questions, the possibility of the state sparing any part of its revenue must be an important element; and if none can be spared, or a productive substitute cannot be found for the tax proposed to be abolished, it will, of course, however undesirable, be necessary to retain it.

A curious instance of native ingenuity, successfully applied to the perpetration of fraud, is to be found in the evidence of Mr. Stark:—In one of the courts of the interior some mock suits were instituted, the proceedings in which were charged with a stamp duty of small amount. The parties contrived to alter the stamps to a higher value; and, after carrying on their litigation for a certain period, they adjusted their dispute without a decree of court, and claimed repayment of the stamp duties, which they actually received, to the full amount of the forgery.

The mode of distributing stamps in India is much the same with that adopted in this country. The stamp vendors receive their supply from the collector; the vendors give security for the stamps, and distribute them to the parties by whom they are required, receiving a per-centage on the sales.

The land assessment and the minor taxes that have been enumerated make up the amount of Indian revenue. A change of taxation is, in any country, a matter of difficult arrangement. Men are very glad to be relieved from imposts which they have been accustomed to pay, but very unwilling to submit to any new burdens in the place of them. In India the force of habit is stronger than in any other part of the world, and the love of money the universal passion. But for the untoward operation of these circumstances, a general

ral revision of the whole system of taxation would be a most desirable measure, tending alike to the improvement of the revenue and the relief of the people. Taxation in India is decidedly unequal. A large class of persons are totally exempt from direct taxation, and that the class most capable of bearing it—the great capitalists. Mr. Sullivan says:—"The meanest labourer in the Madras territories pays a certain proportion of his earnings as an income-tax; but the capitalist, who derives an income of £30,000 or £40,000 from trade, pays no direct tax." It is not easy, by any mode of taxation, to reach such persons. Nothing in the shape of a land tax can extend to them, because they have no land. A tax on property seems almost the only method by which they could be made to contribute to the exigencies of the state. Such an impost, judiciously regulated, may indeed be regarded as the fairest of all modes of taxation, as every man is made to contribute in proportion to his ability. In any country, however, it will incur somewhat more than the average amount of unpopularity which must attend all modes of revenue. In England its inquisitorial nature is considered at variance with our free institutions. In India this characteristic of a property tax would be objected to on different grounds. The natives would be averse to an exposure of the amount of their wealth, not

because

because they felt the inquiry as an invasion of their freedom, but from a fear of exposing themselves to fresh demands; and from that expertness in artifice and concealment which seems an essential part of the native character, they would undoubtedly succeed in keeping out of sight a considerable portion of the property that ought to be submitted to taxation. The measure would excite great discontent and, perhaps, not be very highly productive. It would undoubtedly be evaded to a considerable extent; yet something ought, if possible, to be done, to render the burden of taxation more equal. The subject, however, demands an unusual degree of caution. The people of India are, as Mr. Sullivan observes, "extremely impatient of any new taxation;" and, "a new tax is a very delicate thing."

Whether, therefore, it will be practicable to assist the state, and relieve the poorer classes by any modification of the established system, is doubtful. But, however that may be, it is certain that, in a country so entirely agricultural as India, the land must be looked to as the great source of revenue. The mode in which this revenue is derived bears but little resemblance to what in Europe is understood by a land tax. It rather partakes of the nature of rent. The state may, in fact, be regarded as the owner of the soil, and the assessment levied on the cultivators as the landlord's share

share of the produce. The various modes which have been resorted to for the purpose of securing this share, have been already briefly explained; but it will now be necessary to enter into their merits somewhat more at large.

The origin of these modes must be sought for in a very remote period of time: it is, consequently, involved in great obscurity. It is clear, however, that long previous to the Mahometan conquests, the produce of the land, whether taken in money or in kind, was understood to be shared in certain proportions between the cultivator and the Government. There were thus originally only two parties concerned in the land, those who actually tilled it, and the Government or its representatives. The class of cultivators appears to have been divided into those who were invested with hereditary rights of occupancy, and those who were not. In a country of such extent, divided into different kingdoms, inhabited by people speaking different languages, and distinguished by peculiar customs, some minor diversities might possibly exist; but the great distinction of hereditary and non-hereditary cultivators appears to have existed universally.

The latter class are distinguished, both in Bengal and Madras, by names equivalent to the phrase 'stranger cultivators;' and they are sometimes called 'migratory ryots.' For the purpose of securing

securing the revenue, it has been customary for the Government to call in the aid of such persons to occupy the inferior fields which the hereditary cultivators had left unoccupied. In other cases, they hold as tenants of the hereditary occupiers, either from year to year, or under some special agreement. Under the Madras Presidency, some of these persons seem, by the lapse of time, to have acquired rights of a superior kind. Having been permitted for several generations to occupy certain lands, chiefly those unirrigated in the southern peninsula, which were neglected by the higher class of cultivators, they have succeeded in establishing a prescriptive claim. It is understood, however, that the right thus claimed is not transferable by sale or otherwise.

The superior class of cultivators are distinguished in some parts of India, by a name which signifies 'cultivating their own,' and in others they are denominated 'ancients.' These hold directly of the Government, and their right to the land which they occupy is perpetually subject to the payment of the demands of the public revenue. The payment was made in various ways: sometimes directly to the Government; but more generally the duty of receiving and accounting for it to the State had, when the British dominion was acquired, become hereditary in certain families, and with the heads of those families the State contracted

contracted for its dues. The persons who thus became contractors for the revenues were of varirous ranks and degrees of wealth, from a rajah to a chief cultivator; but all distinctions were confounded under the general name zemindar, which was indiscriminately applied to them; a name which strictly means a landman, but which the British somewhat rashly concluded to be perfectly correspondent with their own term landlord, as meaning proprietor. There is the best evidence to believe that this was an error; that the zemindar was not the owner of the soil, but with a few exceptions the hereditary steward of Government, or contractor for its revenue. From this stewardship or contract he derived a certain profit, generally amounting to about ten or fifteen per cent.; and when, from any cause, his services were declined by the Government, a sum equal to what he thus derived from the collection was paid to him as a compensation.

Confusion has arisen with regard to the rights of the zemindars, from their having been themselves cultivators, which, from the lowest to the highest, they generally were. But, unless the claim of Government on their own fields had been remitted, they would be obliged to account for the amount of revenue assessed upon them, as well as for that assessed upon their neighbours.

To this system there might be, and undoubtedly

edly were, exceptions. In particular instances, in the Northern circars, we found great chieftains bound only to pay a certain tribute to the supreme authority, which the latter was content to receive without recognizing the rights or the obligations of any class under the zemindars. These persons inhabited a hill country, not very easy of access, and still further protected from invasion by a climate deadly to the inhabitants of the plains. They appear at all times to have been, in a great degree, independent, and, as was observed by a witness before the Committee of the House of Commons, to have regarded the Supreme Government much as the Scottish chiefs did the earlier kings of Scotland. They are at present well reconciled to the British Governvernment; but, except in the payment of tribute, there is hardly any communication between the supreme and the subordinate authorities.

If the view which has been taken of the nature of the zemindary right be correct, the permanent settlement, which originated with the Government of Lord Cornwallis, was based upon erroneous principles as to the nature and extent of that right. This is the more extraordinary, as in the discussions which took place previous to the settlement, a sound and just view of the subject seems to have prevailed. It was admitted, that the cultivator had a right to the soil so long as he as he paid the public assessment, which was held to have been fixed beyond the power of the zemindar. It was acknowledged that the zemindar had no right of absolute property in the land itself, and there was no proof "of the existence of such right discernible in his relative situation under the Mogul Government in its best form." Yet the Bengal Government proceeded to recognise the zemindars as the actual proprietors of the land, and to transfer to their keeping, and surrender to their mercy, the rights of all other persons,—rights far more generally admitted and respected, than the right of the zemindar to collect and pay over the revenue of Government. The right of the ryot appears, as expressed by one witness, to be "the greatest right in the country," and "a right which never seems to die." The zemindars have, in many cases, been in a state of constant change. But the right of the ryot is believed to be inalienable. He may quit his land for any period of time, and the cultivation may be assumed by others; but if he or his heir return and reclaim the land, he has only to come to a compromise with the party in possession for the value of the crop on the ground, and his inheritance is restored to him immediately.

The permanent zemindary settlement was a favourite plan of Lord Cornwallis, and undoubtedly originated in benevolent intentions. Its effects, however,

however, have not been such as its projectors anticipated. It was felt, and declared to be "the duty of the ruling power to protect all classes of the people, and more particularly those who from their situations are most helpless;" but the interests of all parties, except of the zemindars, were unfortunately sacrificed.

By the permanent arrangement, the amount of the payment to Government, which had previously been variable, was fixed in perpetuity. But while the Government thus excluded itself from any prospective increase of revenue, by limiting its own demand upon the zemindar, it did not protect the cultivator from oppression, by limiting the demand of the zemindar upon him. A provision was indeed made, that puttahs or leases should be granted; but this was, in fact, annihilating the rights of the superior class of cultivators, who had an hereditary title to their land, and reducing them to the condition of the inferior class, who possessed no hereditary right of occupancy. The zemindar was elevated from the situation of a revenue agent to that of a landlord. He was enjoined to grant leases, but he might demand whatever terms he pleased, and obtain the best that he was able. He even acquired a power to dispose of rights far more ancient, and in the eyes of the people more venerable than his own, and might, to use the words of the Home Government,

ment, " oust even the hereditary ryots from the possession of their lands, when the latter refused to accede to any terms of rent which might be demanded of them, however exorbitant." The local government had anticipated, that the reciprocal wants of the zemindars and cultivators would compel them to enter into just and equitable arrangements; but these flattering expectations were not realised, and it is almost impossible not to feel some surprise that they should have deceived the good and able men by whom they were indulged. The reciprocity, as Lord Hastings observed, is by no means clear. It indeed resembles some other projects of alleged reciprocal advantage, of which it has not unjustly been said, that the reciprocity is all on one side. The zemindar wants cultivators; but in the language of Lord Hastings, " he wants them upon his own terms, and he knows that if he can get rid of the hereditary proprietors who claim a right to terms independent of what he may vouchsafe to give, he will obtain the means of substituting men of his own; and such is the redundancy of the cultivating class, that there will never be a difficulty of procuring ryots ready to engage on terms only just sufficient to secure bare maintenance to the engager." The existence of such a state of things justified his Lordship in affirming that, " if it were the intention of our Regulations to deprive every class

class but the large proprietors, who engaged with Government, of any share in the profits of the land, that effect has been fully accomplished in Bengal." This was not, indeed, the intention of the originators of the permanent zemindary settlement; but it has unhappily been the result of their measures.

In a very few instances some protection was afforded to the ryot. In the Twenty-four Pergunnahs, previously to the introduction of the permanent zemindary settlement, a detailed measurement of the district was made, and a record prepared, specifying the rates to which the public demand on the cultivators was limited, "the settlement being, in fact, ryotwar," and "the zemindars having only the right of collecting what was so settled." Under this system the ryotwar estate has, in many cases, become a property of considerable value; and had the same protection been extended universally, the same effect, modified by local circumstances, would have taken place. But instead of endeavouring to extend this system, the few regulations which seemed to offer some shew of security to the cultivator, were in time replaced by others. Under the Rules of 1793, the form of engagements between the cultivator and zemindar was subjected to the approbation of the collector. This check, in 1812, was dispensed with. At first the zemindars were restricted from fixing the land

land revenue payable by the ryot for any period exceeding ten years. This prohibition was subsequently removed, and doubts having arisen as to the construction of the Regulation, another was passed, explaining that the intent of the former provision was " to declare proprietors of land (meaning the newly-created proprietors, the zemindars) competent to grant leases, even to perpetuity." It is possible that such a permission might ultimately have worked beneficially for a portion of the hapless ryots; but this chance was barred by the addition of the following very important words: " and at any rate which they may deem conducive to their interests."

The introduction of middle men into the collection of rent or revenue always tends to the injury and oppression of those on whom the burden ultimately rests. This system was acted upon to a considerable extent; and though in direct contravention of the law, was tolerated, and finally sanctioned by a provision of indemnity. The rajah of Burdwan, the greatest zemindar under the Bengal Government, his annual contribution amounting to several hundred thousand pounds sterling, distributed his charge into a number of divisions, upon each of which he assessed a fixed sum in perpetuity, always exceeding that for which he himself was liable; and upon condition of the perpetual payment of this increased reserved sum, he he granted the hereditary collection of the land revenue in each division to a new class of sub-zemindars, whom he created for the purpose. Many of these sub-zemindars followed their master's example, by splitting their own primary divisions into secondary ones, and assessing each with a taxed sum in perpetuity, always exceeding that which they were required to pay to the head zemindar. The process of subdivision did not stop even here; for several of these zemindars of the third class divided the portion of the collection which fell to them, upon the same principle as their superiors had done, always taking care that the amount they received was greater than that which they had to pay, and thus a fourth order of zemindars came into existence. The actual contributor to the revenue is thus removed five degrees from the Government to whom he ought to look for justice, and from whose paternal regard he might even hope for some reasonable indulgence. Between him and his final creditor stand four intermediate ones, each armed with the authority of the law; three of them anxious but to secure their stipulated amount of profit, and the fourth only to wring from the cultivator the last anna. His situation may be readily conceived; and it has been stated by a gentleman of the Bengal Civil Service, that "in no part of the country have the ryots been more oppressed than in in this zemindary." The oppression was so gross as at last to call for the interposition of the European officers, to put a stop to the system of demanding from the ryots the most exorbitant rates, and ejecting them from their possessions if they refused to agree to them. That the demands of Government are sometimes light, while those made upon the cultivator are ruinously oppressive, will appear from a fact connected with this zemindary. The Rajah of Burdwan was at one period distressed for money, and sold a portion of his estates. He has since repurchased that which he parted with; and several other estates, upon which he pays yearly forty lacs of rupees, which Mr. Fleming, formerly of the Bengal Civil Service, has heard him acknowledge *is not half of what he collects.* It never could have been the intention of Government to increase the old zemindary allowance of ten or fifteen per cent. to above one hundred, yet this has been the effect of the permanent settlement upon this plan. The case of the Rajah of Burdwan is not a solitary instance. Mr. Holt Mackenzie produced before the Commons' Committee of 1832 a statement, shewing the aggregate Government demand on various estates within certain districts of Bengal, farmed by the Court of Wards, on account of minor and other disqualified zemindars, the rent paid by the farmer, and the profit accruing to the ward.

ward. The result shews a profit on the whole of rather more than a hundred per cent. If some portion of this vast overplus were appropriated to recruit the sinking revenue and the remainder permitted to remain in the pockets of the cultivators, both the state and its subjects would be greatly benefited. This, however, cannot take place, on account of the existing settlement. It must be recollected, that this income is not to be regarded as the rent of a landlord, but the profit of a collector. Never was service so magnificently requited by any Government as the collecting the revenue in India under the permanent settlement.

One estate, particularized in Mr. Mackenzie's paper, is situated in the Twenty-four Pergunnahs, where, as has been already mentioned, the settlement was made upon a detailed measurement. On this property the share of the Government is 6,625 rupees, that of the zemindar 1,976. The profit here, though very ample, falls far short of the average. Of course, there are other instances in which it is very much above the average. One of these is in the district of the Jungle Mehals, where the Government revenue is 3,654 rupees, and the zemindar's profit no less than 16,023.

That the great excess of the receipts of the zemindars over the amount of their payments to Government has been in a great degree occasioned by extortion from the cultivators, cannot admit

admit of doubt. But this, though a very influential cause, has not been the sole one. The permanent settlement was made in a state of great ignorance on the part of Government as to the real amount of the land revenue payable by the cultivators; and in consequence the zemindar's payment was in many instances fixed at a sum quite inadequate. In addition to these causes, a third may be found in the further occupation of land since the settlement. The advantages to be derived from this source were surrendered by the Government as imprudently as unreasonably; for it must be borne in mind, that the Government was the real landlord, and by this proceeding gave away a beneficial right to persons who had no lawful claim to it.

In Madras, one of the evils of the system has been in a great degree avoided, by conforming to a proposal made by Lord Teignmouth, with regard to Bengal, but which unfortunately was not there adopted. That nobleman suggested the propriety of fixing the maximum rates, payable by the cultivators to the zemindar, at those actually assessed when the permanent settlement was introduced. Even this was, perhaps, hardly going far enough, inasmuch as it gave the sanction of Government to all existing cesses, however illegal, and many such had been introduced by the encroaching avarice of the native collectors of the

 revenue.

revenue. But it fixed a limit, beyond which the zemindar could not legally carry his claim, and thus raised a barrier against the introduction of further abuses. Fortunately for the cultivators of Madras, a maximum of contribution was there laid down, by which the sum demandable by the zemindar was restricted to the amount of the rates levied on the cultivated land in the year preceding that of the permanent limitation of the zemindar's payment to the State. The village accounts generally afforded sufficient evidence of these rates; but where they were not ascertainable, the case was decided by reference to the rates payable for other lands of the same description and quality. The consequence was, that the cultivators in Madras were provided with means of defending their rights in the courts of law, to which they have frequently resorted with success. In Bengal, unfortunately, these rights were not thus ascertained and recognized, and the power of the zemindar was unlimited.

The zemindary system was not only continued and rendered permanent where it had previously existed, but in some instances was introduced where a different system had prevailed. In Madras, and in a great portion of the provinces of Bahar and Benares, there were associations of cultivators, holding their lands sometimes in severalty, sometimes on a joint common tenure. With regard

regard to these, two courses were open, and the respective Governments differed in their views as to the more eligible. The one was to introduce a stranger to the office of zemindar, the other to invest with it some of the inhabitants of the village. The latter plan was adopted by the Government of Bengal, the former by that of Madras, and both have been productive of inconvenience. Under the Bengal system, the office of zemindar was sometimes imposed upon an individual against his will. He was made liable for the payment of that which was due from others as well as from himself: and as no distinction was made between the ancient rights of possession, and the newly-acquired, and often reluctantly accepted ones, attached to the collection of the revenue, his ancient inheritance was liable to be brought to sale by the default of others. Sometimes the ruin produced by individual defalcation was more extensive, as when it happened that the zemindary was held in common by the cultivators; a dispute between the coparceners might throw the payment of the revenue into arrear; and in such a case, the whole of the joint property—the right in the soil, as well as the zemindary right—the rights of those who had contributed their due proportion to the revenue, as well as of those who had committed default—might be passed into new hands by virtue of a sale under the orders

orders of Government. The following case, illustrative of the consequences of this system, is given in Mr. Campbell's able paper on the subject.

"A very extraordinary instance of this kind occurred in 1834, in the case of the 'Tuppa of Muneer,' a zemindary held by a community of Rajpoots, assessed with a jumma of 13,514 rupees, payable into the public treasury. Two only of this body, from some dispute with the rest, refused to pay up a small portion of this sum due from their fields, and an arrear consequently accrued to the extent of 1,014 rupees. The others offered payment of the sum due on account of their more extensive fields to the amount of the remaining balance of 12,500 rupees; but as the regulations for the permanent settlement do not provide for any summary mode of adjusting such disputes, and on any arrear accruing hold the entire zemindary responsible, prohibiting most rigidly a division so long as such arrear is due; this tender was necessarily refused by the collector, who proceeded to sell the entire zemindary for the arrear due actually by only two of the coparceners. It produced at first 99,000 rupees; but as it was discovered that the purchaser was one of the community, all of whom, though not actually such, are, in the eye of the law, considered defaulters, and therefore excluded by the Regulations from making a purchase of what the code

code deems their own property, this first sale was cancelled, and the zemindary being put up again was bought by a low-caste stranger for 50,000 rupees. The Rajpoot zemindars upon this instituted a suit in the Provincial Court to annul the second sale, and obtained a decree declaring it illegal; but the Company's Supreme Court at Calcutta, on appeal, upheld the second sale, upon the ground of a balance having actually been due from the zemindary. To this decision the Rajpoots still refused submission; and Mr. Melville, whose duty it became to enforce it, submitted to the Bengal Government, whether its character in the province for consideration in enforcing its dues was not deeply involved on the occasion; adding, that himself as judge, and the collector, Mr. Barlow, felt reluctant to be instruments to carry into execution a measure which they conceived to be severe upon a large body of hereditary and respectable zemindars, and at variance with the mild and liberal spirit of the Government they had the honour to serve. As the best means of obviating this, he suggested that the Government should obtain, by negotiation, the surrender of the zemindary from the second purchaser, and this was at last effected by the Government paying to him no less a sum than 2,06,987 rupees, whence deducting his purchase-money of 50,000 rupees, there remained a sum of

rupees

rupees 1,56,987. On payment of their respective proportions of this immense sum, the original Rajpoot zemindars were allowed to resume possession of their fields, and this indulgence was extended even to those who were unable to pay their proportion to this large capital, on their consenting to pay to Government interest at six per cent. on their several proportions of it, as an additional assessment on their lands for ever."

This extraordinary transaction scarcely requires comment; but it receives a very proper and spirited one from Mr. Campbell. He says: "To recover an arrear of only 1,014 rupees due actually by two persons alone, against whom, under the regulations of the permanent settlement, no means could be taken to enforce it individually, the whole property, both in the land revenue and in the land itself, of the entire community (the rest of whom had repeatedly tendered their dues), was here brought to sale by public auction. The court of highest jurisdiction in Bengal, bound apparently by the same regulations, confining responsibility to the entire community, to the exclusion altogether of individual rights, seem even to have been obliged to uphold this act of injustice, and when the Government found it impossible to overlook it, as brought to their notice by their officers, who declined to be made the instruments of such a proceeding, they were constrained

strained to put into the pocket of a speculator at auction no less a sum than 1,56,987 rupees, which immense amount, or its equivalent, being equal to twelve years' land revenue, they actually took out of the purses of their own cultivating zemindars, most of whom owed them absolutely nothing, and of whom two alone owed them only the trifling sum of 1,014 rupees, or not so much as one-hundredth part of that exacted."

If any further comment be necessary, it is furnished by the effect of the transaction upon the people, which is thus stated:

"The feelings of the people on this occasion, as represented by the officer deputed by Government to negotiate for the surrender of the zemindary by the intrusive purchaser, who did not venture to approach his new speculation, deserve notice. 'Muneer,' says he, 'may contain 8,000 or 10,000 Rajpoot youths; but the question of sale unfortunately did not find its limits here. There were, probably, 60,000 ready to make common cause with them.' One of the coparceners, with a tone to which this officer's ears had never been accustomed, demanded, 'If Government are determined to sell our lands, why dishonour the caste by a sale to a gootum? Our chief is the Rajah of Buleah, and he is a rich man;' and it was added, that the whole of these village zemindars 'seemed to have lost their natural civility of manner,

ner, common respect to the European officers, and proper feelings of honesty to Government, from some extraordinary and unintelligible interpretation of the Regulations which were only designed for their safety.'"

Such are the results of legislating without a proper regard to established usages and institutions.

In Madras, the course adopted was in an equal or a greater degree at variance with the feelings of the people, and the consequences were not more happy. In the Northern Circars, indeed, there was an ancient aristocracy, to whom the people looked up as their hereditary superiors, and through whom the Supreme Government could most conveniently realise its revenue. But in the other districts to which the permanent settlement was extended, a novel and not very happy attempt was made to create an aristocracy by public auction. A cluster of villages, called a mootah or zemindary, was put up to sale, and the highest bidder became the new hereditary zemindar or moohtahdar, the terms being synonimous. The Government revenue had been previously assessed, not upon each field, nor upon each village, but upon the whole mootah or zemindary, and for this the new speculator in nobility was held accountable. There was under this system no bond of connection between the cultivators and the purchasers of the zemindary right, who were totally unconnected

nected with the land. They were monied men, desirous of elevating themselves by their wealth into the rank of Rajahs. *Parvenus* are proverbially haughty and overbearing; and it is represented, and may readily be believed, that the ryots suffered considerable annoyance from these speculators. In consequence, however, of the provision made on their behalf, they frequently succeeded in vindicating their rights, and were generally, in the course of time, emancipated altogether from the dominion of the newly-created zemindars, most of whom gradually failed, and with their families became involved in distress.

The zemindars generally appear to have been distinguished by improvidence and want of thrift. In Madras, they are represented as having mismanaged their zemindaries so completely, that in the Northern Districts only one remained in a prosperous condition, their zemindaries having been, for the most part, transferred to the Government officers as security for the payment of the revenue, and that they might be retrieved from the disorder into which they had fallen. In the Company's jaghire, in 1826, the zemindaries were reduced to 651 villages, paying a fixed jumma of 2,97,940 rupees; while lands had reverted to Government to the extent of 1,217 villages, paying a revenue of 4,88,960 rupees. In the Salem district, a similar result followed. In the Dindigul district,

district, the zemindary settlement was introduced in 1804-5; but in 1806-7 the lands, with scarcely any exception, reverted to the Government. In this district, however, the failure is ascribed to over-assessment. In Bengal, the sales in the years 1796 and 1797 extended to zemindaries assessed at the sum of Sicca Rupees 14,18,765; in 1797 and 1798, to others assessed at the still larger amount of Rupees 22,74,076; and in 1815 it was estimated, that "probably one-third, or rather one-half, of the landed property in the province of Bengal may have been transferred by public sale, on account of the arrears of revenue." Since that time the number of sales has diminished; but in some years it is still considerable.

These sales afford some evidence that the zemindars have not been greatly benefited by the present of the right in the soil made to them by the Government. Their unthriftiness has prevented their profiting by it. But it has not been the zemindar alone who has suffered from the sale. By a very extraordinary regulation under the Bengal Presidency, the sale of a zemindary for arrears cancelled all existing engagements between the zemindar and the cultivator, and left the purchaser at liberty to demand what terms he pleased. He was required, indeed, to conform to the local rates; but as these were unascertained, the limitation was a dead letter. By a subsequent

quent regulation, the purchaser was invested with a summary power of ejecting any of the cultivators. This power was at a later period withdrawn; but it continued for twenty-two years, and was exercised to a frightful extent. Even in the regulation which put an end to this grievance, it is laid down as "a general and fundamental principle of the revenue system" in Bengal, that the public sale of the zemindar's tenures for arrears annuls all engagements derived from him or his predecessors. This is not only a hardship upon the ryot, but operates as a direct discouragement to improved cultivation.

The permanent settlement has rendered little substantial benefit to the zemindar; it has, in a great degree, annihilated the rights of the ryots; but to one class of people its operation has been highly beneficial—it has materially promoted the interests of the followers of the law. Within two years after the permanent settlement was established in Bengal, thirty thousand suits which had arisen from the difficulties created by that settlement were depending in the district of Burdwan alone. The sale of the single Rajpoot zemindary of Muneer, already mentioned, gave rise to 1,060 law-suits. The foundations of all rights having been violently broken up, litigation in consequence multiplied and abounded. The courts were choked up with business, the amount of which

which the most indefatigable exertions of the judges were inadequate to reduce. What is called the permanent settlement may, indeed, be regarded, in Bengal especially, as having unsettled every thing, and settled nothing but the Government assessment.

Notwithstanding these obvious evils, attempts have been made to repeat the unsuccessful experiment of a permanent settlement, by extending it to the western provinces. These were, in the first instance, frustrated by the objections of Mr. R.W. Cox and Mr. Henry St. George Tucker, who were appointed commissioners for carrying the plan into effect. It is remarkable that both these gentlemen were advocates for the system; but on being deputed to superintend its establishment in an untried spot, they perceived that objections existed to its introduction, and these they had the manliness and candour freely to point out. But, notwithstanding their representations, the Bengal Government persisted in its determination to introduce the permanent settlement; and the commissioners, finding their views thus at variance with those of the supreme authority, felt themselves called upon to resign. The Home Government appear to have taken a view of the subject more just, calm, and statesman-like, than that of the local Government, and, in the words of Mr. Sullivan, "uniformly evinced, throughout the whole

whole correspondence on this grand question, fully as strong an anxiety that the rights of individuals should not be infringed, as that the interests of the State should not be compromised by a premature discussion." A termination was put to the proposed extension of the system in 1817, when the Board of Control and the Court of Directors, after ample discussion, finally agreed upon the following points :—

" That the system of 1793, though originating in the most enlightened views and the most benevolent motives, and though having produced considerable good, has, nevertheless, been attended in the course of its operation with no small portion of evil to the people, for whose happiness it was intended.

" That the same views and motives which dictated the original introduction of the permanent settlement twenty-five years ago, would not, *after the experience which had been had of it,* justify the immediate introduction of the same system into provinces for which a system of revenue administration is yet to be settled.

" That the creation of an artificial class of intermediate proprietors between the Government and the cultivators of the soil, where a class of intermediate proprietors does not exist in the native institutions of the country, would be highly inexpedient.

" That

"That no conclusive step ought to be taken towards a final settlement of the yet unsettled provinces, until it shall have been examined, and, if possible, ascertained by diligent research and comparison of collected testimonies, as well as by accurate survey of the lands to be settled, how far the principle of a system, which would bring the Government into immediate contact with the great body of the people, can be practically and usefully applied to them."

This decision was dictated by a sound policy. The attempt to create a landed aristocracy was, from first to last, based upon erroneous views. Had it been practicable, it could not be effected without the destruction of a mass of private rights, which it was the duty of the law to protect, instead of subverting. The observations of Mr. Campbell on this point are just and convincing. "In India," says he, "where the only aristocracy connected with the land are the mere hereditary farmers-general or contract-agents of the Government, and the soil itself is invariably occupied by a numerous class of petty proprietary cultivators, it was obviously impracticable to introduce the European theory of landlord and tenant without an infraction of individual rights. It never ought to have been, nor can it now even justly be made a question for consideration or decision, whether in India it be politic to give the preference to great

great or to small holders of land. The law and usage of the country have immemorially and irrevocably determined the right in the soil to be vested in particular classes. Whatever may be the extent or value of such right, the smallest, no less than the greatest, tenure should be held inviolably sacred; and the rights of millions of field proprietors to hold on defined terms, directly of the State, never can be abrogated for a mere theoretical improvement in the administration of the land revenue, without an act of the most sweeping confiscation ever hazarded by a civilized government. It was clearly the duty of a just government anxiously to protect all existing rights; and, by defining its demand on the possessor of each tenure holding immediately of the State, to maintain every class in its respective situation, and to ensure the benefit of any remission or reduction in its land revenue to those who pay it, instead of allowing it to be intercepted by its intermediate revenue contractor, the zemindar."

But had there been no previous rights in the way, the attempt, suddenly to call into existence an aristocracy, whose claims were based neither on property nor ancient usage, would have failed. The plan, indeed, was no where distinguished by even the semblance of success, except in the districts where the zemindar's authority was continued in its ancient line; and in these cases that

 part

part of the plan which subjected the zemindar's right to sale, in case of default, was productive of the most serious mischief. Some sales which took place in the Ganjam district, by which the rights of an ancient family there were transferred to some foreign purchasers, led to an actual rebellion. Troops were employed to suppress it; but ultimately Government entered into a negociation, by which the zemindary was restored to the family, and the disturbances immediately ceased. Under the native powers it was not the practice to sell the zemindar's right. Government sometimes assumed the temporary collection of the revenue, and sometimes transferred it to some other member of the zemindar's family. The zemindar himself was subject even to corporal punishment, but his right was never brought to sale. The enforcement of such a system consequently outraged the feelings of all classes where the institution was ancient; and the description of persons whom the sales frequently introduced to the exercise of the zemindary authority, was little calculated to allay the feelings of irritation excited by the forcible expulsion of an old family. The best of them were capitalists, who entered on the office of zemindar in the spirit in which they embarked in a mercantile speculation, and whose only object was, of course, to make the largest profit upon their outlay. They were often unacquainted with the habits, the feelings,

ings, the wants, and even the language of the cultivators—were frequently non-resident—in which case their interests and those of the people were entrusted to agents no better informed than themselves. But there were purchasers who were destitute even of the recommendation of commercial respectability. It is represented, that banyans, money-lenders, menial servants of Europeans, vakeels, and other retainers of the courts of law, seized the opportunity of elevating themselves in society, by purchasing into this new aristocracy; and in what manner the unlimited power of a zemindar would, in such hands, be exercised, need not be pointed out. It is sufficient merely to state the fact, to shew how completely the lofty designs of Lord Cornwallis were frustrated. He never contemplated the formation of a landed aristocracy out of the very dregs and refuse of society; yet this was, in some degree, the effect of his favourite measure, and for such consumers as these have the producers of agricultural wealth been divested of their rights, and deprived for ever of the power of accumulation.

It was observed by the local Government in 1821, that, "looking to the character and conduct of many of the zemindars in Bengal, it might well be questioned whether the rent drawn by them from their zemindaries was less a tax upon the country than if the amount were collected on

 the

the account of the Government." This is put more cautiously, and with more deference to the zemindars than the circumstances of the case warrant. The matter is too clear to admit of question. It is beyond all doubt that the revenue drawn by the zemindars on their own account is as much a tax as if it were collected for Government. It is equally certain that it is far more oppressively levied than it would be in the hands of Government. And this vast revenue is generally expended as worthily as it is obtained. It goes, according to Mr. Thackeray, almost entirely to feed the idle and unproductive—footmen, peons, dancing-girls, and Brahmins; it is wasted in silly and ostentatious display, in tasteless and debasing luxury, in superstitious benefactions, and in vice. Thus the grinding process to which the laborious cultivator is subjected, ends in ministering to the appetites of the idle and depraved.

No country under such a system can be either wealthy or prosperous, and in the provinces where it exists the permanent settlement will long continue to operate as a serious check upon the progress of improvement. In other countries, the landlord takes an interest in the improvement of his property. In India, this feeling appears to be unknown among those who have been imprudently invested with the rank and authority of landlords. Mr. Newnham, when examined before

fore the Committee of the House of Commons in 1832, was asked, "Has the zemindar any such property in land as ever induces him to invest capital in the improvement of it? Are there any instances of a zemindar building houses for the ryots, or advancing money for irrigation or fencing?" The answer was: "Many persons advocate the zemindary cause by alleging outlay of capital; but it is seldom more than a mere current loan, repayable at a very high interest, or, which is worse, the repayment in commodity at a very much lower price than the market price; but as for any permanent outlay of capital in digging wells and making tanks, I fear that there are very few instances of zemindars laying out capital in that way. The great improvements in the country take place from the junction of the ryots in different labours; at least I have seen them making bridges across rivers, sinking wells, making watercourses from tanks, or collections of water, and undertaking many important works of that kind." The same gentleman thus speaks of the condition of the ryots as affected by the system under which they live, in answer to a question relating to their means of cultivating their lands: "I fear that borrowed capital is the general character of the ryot; but where he is in full possession of his rights and privileges, and has security, there you will find *that* capital in his possession, and

and it is shewn both in his own comforts and in the goodness of his farming stock; for instance, there is a material difference between a pair of half-starved inferior-sized bullocks, which are probably not worth eight rupees the pair, and another man ploughing with a pair of fine bullocks, for which he gives from twenty to twenty-five rupees each." Improvement cannot be effected without capital, nor can it be carried to any great extent if that capital be furnished on terms extortionate and oppressive. The zemindary settlement is, in this point of view, as objectionable as in every other. It tends to retard the increase of public wealth, no less than to destroy the individual comfort of the cultivators.

The permanent settlement extends to the provinces of Bengal, Behar, Orissa, and Benares, with the exception of Cuttack. Under the Madras presidency its general failure has considerably reduced its limits, Government having, in many cases, repurchased the tenure. In addition to the greater portion of the five Northern Circars, it is reported to extend to about a third of the Salem and Chingleput districts; to the Pollams scattered through several provinces to the northward, westward, and southward of Madras; to a few insulated portions of the Dindigul districts, supposed to fall short of a tenth of the whole; and a small part of the southern division of Arcot, consisting

consisting of some of the Company's ancient lands near Cuddalore. No part of the territory subject to the Presidency of Bombay was ever under the permanent settlement.

It has been seen that the attempt to introduce this system into the Western Provinces was delayed, in the first instance, by the objections of the commissioners, Mr. H. St. George Tucker and Mr. R. W. Cox (which, however, were directed not against the principle but the time and local circumstances of its application), and that it was finally suspended by a solemn decision of the home authorities. A large portion of these provinces was brought under a form of the zemindary system somewhat resembling that of the permanent settlement, but limited to a term of years. This temporary settlement was made with a class of persons called (as in the lower provinces) proprietors. It is admitted, however, by one of the warmest advocates of the plan, that "the first settlement" was "made, in very many instances, to the exclusion of those who were supposed to be the proprietors, and the lands let to farmers." He adds, indeed, "but still, in a very great many cases, those *supposed to be* the proprietors were in possession, and paying revenue to the Government."

What degree of care was taken to ascertain the correspondence of this supposition with the fact is not stated; but the gentleman from whose evidence

dence the passage just quoted is extracted, apparently did not think it necessary that any great labour should be devoted to the enquiry, as in a subsequent part of his evidence he says, "I do not think it at all necessary to enter into a minute examination of rights and claims in every case, because, according to my experience, *that would be endless;* but you should do that only in cases where rights are set up, and where a call is made for enquiry." It would seem, indeed, that this was the system acted on; as another witness, Mr. Newnham, says, "Those who came forward as zemindars were recognized as zemindars; and in the villages in which zemindars had not been forthcoming, or withheld from engagement, agreements were made with farmers who had power of collection." And on being asked, "What inducement could any person who was a zemindar have for not coming forward?" He answers, "Because he had the responsibility of a revenue without any profit, where the assessment was too high." And it is afterwards stated, that in certain territories "it was as high as it could be with any sort of justice." Yet there were persons found where the lawful zemindar concealed himself, to render themselves accountable for this heavy assessment—calculating, of course, upon some personal advantage, which could only be realised by extracting from the ryots something beyond that

amount

amount, which was as large " as it well could be with any sort of justice." Had the permanent settlement taken place, this rapacious intruder would have become the lord of the soil. As it is, there has been quite enough of confusion and mischief, and sales have taken place which are inexplicable both in their nature and their results. It seems altogether uncertain whether or not any property was acquired under the zemindary settlement; if any, it appears equally doubtful what it is; and the rights conveyed by the sales which took place are shrouded in mystery. The following questions and answers extracted from the examination of Mr. Holt Mackenzie, 1832, are too important and instructive to admit of abridgment:

" Q. The Committee are informed, in the districts about Bareilly, and the neighbouring districts, leases for three years were granted to persons called zemindars, and instances occurred of rent running in arrear in that short period, and of sales having taken place of some beneficial interest that the zemindar under those circumstances was supposed to possess; are you aware of it?—A. Such sales took place extensively in many of the districts; and in all, more or less, in which the printed Regulations were in force. The tenure sold was sometimes the same with that of the Bengal zemindars. In other cases, the persons recorded as responsible for the Government revenue

nue clearly stood forward as the mere representatives of a community. In some, though standing in that relation originally, they contrived to secure for themselves exclusively the profit arising out of the settlement with Government; and generally, though there might be some coparceners, the two or three who came forward had their names recorded by our collectors, and stood upon the Government books as if they were the only zemindars, while they were merely members of a large community, having equal rights.

" Q. Whenever they fell in arrear, you sold them all?—A. *Nobody can tell what was sold in such cases. It is a puzzle to this day to say what was sold.*

" Q. What state of things has been produced by those proceedings?—A. Great confusion has resulted; the purchasers generally claiming to have acquired a complete property in the villages sold, according to the Bengal rules relative to joint estates; and I am afraid that the same thing has occurred in Behar, and still more in Benares, where there are many village communities of whom the persons who appeared upon our books were the mere representatives. Mr. Duncan, indeed, prepared special rules for Benares that ought to have preserved the inferior holders; but unhappily his system was confounded very much with the Bengal system: and I believe that the courts have ruled

ruled that the sale of a village for Government arrears due by one recorded as a proprietor, absolutely conveyed to the purchaser all the rights of property in that village.

"Q. What has been the effect of this?—A. *Infinite mischief. Greater injustice, indeed, no Government ever inflicted upon a country.*"

Such a state of things could not, of course, be permitted to continue. In the Western Provinces, the process of sale has latterly been nearly suspended. In 1821, a special commission was appointed to enquire into the sales that had taken place, and into the rights of all persons and classes in the villages sold. Subsequently, similar powers were extended to the Revenue Commissioners, who were authorized to set aside sales in all cases of hardship, giving compensation to *bonâ fide* purchasers, and to annul illegal and fraudulent sales without compensation. It was further intended to form a settlement based upon a careful census and survey; but these have proceeded slowly.

To remedy the evils arising from delay, the late Governor General recommended the renewal on a summary revision of existing engagements at an enhanced jumma, and for protracted periods. In the event of this proposal being approved, he suggested the following principles as the groundwork of proceeding—that the extended leases should not fall short of fifteen, nor exceed twenty years

years—that the detailed survey should go on during this period preparatory to a settlement on the more accurate data which it would furnish—that the arrangement should be optional, the collectors proposing it to the landholders, leaving them perfectly at liberty to adopt the alternative of abiding the result of the detailed settlement at the most early period at which it might be in the power of Government to effect it, in preference to the certainty of being subjected to one uniform demand only for a definite period.

Whether this or any other plan be adopted, two points should be carefully kept in view—to prejudice no existing right, and to create no new one. The scenes which have been acted in a part of the unsettled provinces must not be repeated, and no labour must be thought too great to ascertain the precise nature of all existing tenures.

Some popular disturbances, which took place in the Western Provinces, and especially at Bareilly, have been ascribed to the non-fulfilment of the intention of extending the permanent settlement to those provinces. Looking to the spot in which these commotions occurred, and recollecting the facts stated in the evidence of Mr. Mackenzie, some doubt will naturally arise as to the alleged cause. Mr. Trant, indeed, who assigns this cause, at the same time admits that the disturbances arose, in the first place, out of the imposition

sition of a police tax. Mr. Fortescue, who does not deny that they had some connection with the postponement of the permanent settlement, considers the wish for that settlement to have been confined to the zemindars. He believes, moreover, that there were other causes operating (as Mr. Trant admits), and inasmuch as the disturbances were connected with the non-introduction of a permanent settlement, he looks upon them to have been instigated and fomented by those who had an especial interest in the subject. This appears to be the most natural and probable solution of the matter, and being corroborated on one important point by the testimony of an adversary, it may be regarded as the true one.

In the permanently settled provinces, we have committed ourselves too far to be able to retrace our steps; but in all future proceedings sound policy seems to dictate the discouragement of the zemindary system in any shape, as far as is consistent with rights established by immemorial custom, or sanctioned by positive law. It is a bad system for the cultivator—it is equally bad for the Government. It has been suggested, that under a zemindary system the rights of the ryots might be ascertained and protected. This, however, would be to combine two systems instead of adopting one; and as one of the recommendations of the zemindary plan is its apparent simplicity

plicity and facility of application, such an appendage to it as the proposal implies, can scarcely find favour in the eyes of those who regard it as an instrument for collecting the revenue with the smallest portion of trouble. But if the rights of the ryots be admitted (and they are clearer than the rights of any other persons in India), on what principle can we justify the withdrawing from them the natural protection of Government?

The observations of Sir Thomas Munro on the question are replete with sound vigorous sense. He says, "If in place of lowering the assessment and letting landed property rise in the natural way, we want to have great landlords raised at once where none exist, and for this purpose create zemindars and turn over to each of them some hundreds of ryots, we should commit a gross injustice; because we should enable the zemindar in time to degrade the ryots from the rank of tenants in chief to that of tenants at will, and often to that of mere cultivators or labourers. We say that we leave the ryots free to act and to make their own terms with the zemindars or renters, and that if they were wronged the courts will protect them. We put them out of sight, deliver them over to a superior, and then we tell them that they are free to make their own terms, and that there are courts to secure their rights. *But with what pretence of justice can we place them*

under

under any set of men, to make terms for their property, and to defend it against them in courts of law? They have no superior but Government; they are tenants in chief, and ought not to be obliged to make terms except with Government. But it is said that the zemindar does not infringe their rights, because he has no authority to demand more than the dues of Government, as regulated by the usage of the country, and that if the parties be left to themselves things will find their proper level. They will find the level which they have found in Bengal and several districts under this Government, and *which the weak always find when they are left to contend with the strong*. The question is, whether we are to continue the country in its natural state, occupied by a great body of independent ryots, and to enable them, by a lighter assessment, to rise gradually to the rank of landlords, or whether we are to place the country in an artificial state, by dividing it into villages or larger districts among a new class of landholders, who will inevitably, at no distant period, by the subdivision of their new property, fall to the level of ryots; while the ryots will, at the same time, have sunk from the rank of independent tenants in chief to that of sub-tenants and cultivators. It is, whether we are to raise the landholders we have, or to create a new set, and see them fall." The actual working

working of the system in Madras is described in another part of the minute from which the last quotation is made. "There is no analogy whatever between the landlord of England and his tenants, and the moohtahdar or new village zemindar of this country and his ryots. In England the landlord is respected by the farmer as his superior; here a zemindar has no such respect, for the principal ryots of most villages regard him as not more than their equal, and often as their inferior. He is often the former potail, or head ryot of the village; but he is frequently some petty shopkeeper, or merchant, or some adventurer, or public servant out of employ. Whichever of these he is, he has usually very little property. He has none for the improvement of the village; but, on the contrary, looks to the village as the means of improving his own circumstances. The ryots, by being placed under him, sink from the rank of tenants of the Government to that of tenants of an individual. They are transferred from a superior, who has no interest but in their protection and welfare, to one whose interest it is to enlarge his own property at the expense of their's; who seeks, by every way, however unjustifiable, to get into his own hands all the best lands of the village, and whose situation affords him many facilities in depriving the ancient possessors of theirs. The ryots are jealous of a man whose

new

new power and influence they have so much to fear. They frequently combine, in order to keep down the cultivation, and force him, for their own security, to give up the village. And hence it has happened, that on the one side the opposition of the ryots, and on the other the oppression of the new zemindar, have, in many instances, caused villages which were flourishing, and moderately assessed, to revert to the circar, from inability to pay their assessment." Never, indeed, were good intentions so lamentably frustrated as they have been by this system; and to attempt to make it universal throughout our Indian possessions, might shake the security of our empire. The system is radically vicious. Where, however, it already exists we must tolerate it; but it would be a most fatal error, as all experience shews, to endeavour to extend it. Again, quoting the words of Sir Thomas Munro, when speaking of the effects produced by the forcible introduction of this system: "Such an innovation would be much more fatal to the old rights of property than conquest by a foreign enemy; for such a conquest, though it overthrew the Government, would leave the people in their former condition. But this internal change, the village revolution, changes every thing, and throws both influence and property into new hands. It deranges the order of society; it depresses one class of men for the sake of raising another; it weakens the respect and authority of ancient offices and institutions; and the local administration, conducted by their means, is rendered much more difficult. It is time that we should learn that neither the face of a country, its property, or its society, are things that can be suddenly improved by any contrivances of our's, though they may be greatly injured by what we mean for their good; that we should take every country as we find it, and not rashly attempt to regulate its landed property, either in its accumulation or division; that whether it be held by a great body of ryots, or by a few zemindars, or by a mixture of both, our business is not with its distribution, but with its protection; and that if while we protect, we assess it moderately, and leave it to its natural course, it will, in time, flourish, and assume that form which is most suitable to the condition of the people."

The observations of the same distinguished person on the general principles which should guide those who undertake the high task of improving the condition of India, are no less just and instructive: "We are now," he says, "masters of a very extensive empire, and we should endeavour to improve and secure it by a good internal administration. Our experience is too short, to judge what rules are best calculated for the purpose. It is only within the last thirty years that we have begun

begun to acquire any practical knowledge; a longer period must probably elapse before we can ascertain what is best. *Such a period is as nothing in the existence of a people;* but we act as if this were as limited as the life of an individual. We proceed, in a country of which we know little or nothing, as if we knew every thing, and as if every thing must be done now and nothing could be done hereafter. We feel our ignorance of Indian revenue and the difficulties arising from it: and instead of seeking to remedy it, by acquiring more knowledge, we endeavour to get rid of the difficulty by precipitately making permanent settlements, which relieve us from the troublesome task of minute or accurate investigation, and which are better adapted to perpetuate our ignorance than to protect the people. We must not be led away by fanciful theories, founded on European models, which will inevitably end in disappointment. We must not too hastily declare any rights permanent, lest we give to one class what belongs to another. We must proceed patiently, and as our knowledge of the manners and customs of the people and the nature and resources of the country increase, frame gradually, from the existing institutions, such a system as may advance the prosperity of the country, and be satisfactory to the people. The knowledge most necessary for this end is that of the landed property and its assessment; for the land is not only the great source of the public revenue, but on its fair and moderate assessment depend the comfort and happiness of the people." In another place, Sir Thomas Munro adverts to the mistakes which have been committed, in a manner which should operate as a warning against indiscreet zeal for the future: "Our great error in this country, during a long course of years, has been too much precipitation in attempting to better the condition of the people with hardly any knowledge of the means by which it was to be accomplished, and, indeed, without seeming to think that any other than good intentions were necessary. It is a dangerous system of government, in a country of which our knowledge is very imperfect, to be constantly urged by the desire of settling every thing permanently, to do every thing in a hurry, and, in consequence, wrong; and, *in our zeal for permanency, to put the remedy out of our reach.* The ruling vice of our government is innovation; and its innovation has been so little guided by a knowledge of the people, that, *though made after what was thought by us to be a mature discussion, must appear to them as little better than mere caprice.*" Such observations, which would scarcely at any time be unseasonable, are peculiarly deserving of notice in an age, the ruling vice of which is that which Sir Thomas Munro ascribes

to

to the English authority in India—innovation. The great error of concluding that laws and institutions which produce good effects in one country, will, therefore, produce good effects in all other countries, must be carefully avoided; and if it be necessary to bear this in mind with regard to that which has been tried, though under different circumstances, the necessity is still more imperious with reference to systems altogether untried, and which have not the sanction of even a partial or local experience. If we would benefit the people of India, we must legislate for them as they are, and not as theorists conceive they ought to be. We must respect their local usages and institutions, wherever they are not productive of positive evil; and even where they are, they must be removed with a gentle hand. The general habit of the people is submission to authority, and it will be our own fault if they learn a different lesson. If we are content to derive a moderate revenue from the land, and to abstain from all interference with existing rights, except to protect them, the people will advance in wealth and happiness, and the British dominion take root in their interests and feelings. But if fanciful schemes, concocted in the closets of speculators and sciolists, framed with an ostentatious disregard of local peculiarities, claiming an universal applicability, and, like a patent medicine, "warranted

ranted to keep good in any climate," are imposed upon a people little addicted to novelty, in place of the institutions to which they have been accustomed, which have grown with the growth of the nation and become part of its very essence, discontent, disgust, and confusion will be inevitable, and the final results may be such as no friend, either to India or England, can wish to contemplate. But while we discourage such a mischievous activity, we must not take refuge in indolence and supineness. It is at once our interest and our duty to settle nothing permanently till it can be settled in a manner satisfactory to the people; but it is also our interest and our duty to spare no labour that may be necessary to enable us to acquire that minute knowledge of Indian institutions which is indispensable to a satisfactory settlement. Of two plans we must not give the preference to one solely on the ground of its involving less trouble than the other. Nothing must be left to chance or accident, nor must the preservation of any class of rights be suffered to depend upon the clamorous violence with which they may happen to be urged. The weak, as well as the strong, the silent as well as the loud, the ignorant as well as the informed, must be protected; and as we must not be parsimonious of labour, so neither must we be impatient of the consumption of time. The work to be accomplished is not that

of

of a day or a year, and provided no time is wasted, it will, if well done, be done sufficiently early.

By an adherence to such rules, we may guard against the recurrence of evils similar to those the existence of which there is reason to lament under the permanent settlement. To correct those evils which have already arisen is a less direct and a far more difficult task. It has been justly said, that "the practical difficulty of adjusting the relation of the zemindar and the ryot, after an assignment to the former of all he can gain by the destruction of the latter, is of the most serious nature." Yet it must be remembered that the fault was with the Government and not with the people, and therefore the former is bound to do all within its power to mitigate the evils which it cannot entirely remove. Little of a general nature can be done, but something may be accomplished in detail; and this the Home Government have evinced a disposition to perform, manifesting that laudable regard to the interests of the people committed to its care, and that accurate perception of the true nature of those interests, which from the commencement of its rule have been the leading characteristics of the policy of the Company. It has hitherto been judged inexpedient to interfere, so long as the zemindar is punctual in fulfilling his engagements with the Government; but the Home Authority has directed, that

in

in the event of arrears accruing, and a sale being deemed necessary (except in cases where the sacrifice on account of purchase money would be very great) the zemindary tenure should be bought on the part of the Government, and a settlement made on the ryotwar principle. Under the Bengal presidency this instruction has not been acted upon to any extent. Under the Madras presidency, it has been already stated, that a large portion of the country, formerly settled under the zemindary tenure, has reverted to Government.

The purchase and resumption of the rights imprudently conceded to the zemindars is undoubtedly the least exceptionable method of remedying the evil of their existence; but a serious objection lies against it, arising from the outlay of money required to carry it into effect to any considerable extent. For this reason Mr. Campbell suggests that it would be desirable, without changing the existing law rendering the zemindary tenure saleable for arrears, in practice to suspend its operation, and on an arrear, accruing, to attach and continue the attachment of the land revenue, and to introduce a ryotwar field assessment. This plan may, probably, be adopted with some benefit where the purchase of the right by Government is impracticable or inexpedient; but as the suspension of the zemindars' right would be only temporary, it does not appear very easy to see

how

how we should be legally justified in interfering between the ryots and himself, except upon the principle that extreme evils justify the application of extreme remedies, which, if acted upon, might carry us much farther than Mr. Campbell's proposal. Whenever the zemindars' right can be altogether annihilated (except in cases of ancient claim), this course will be preferable. The mischief arising from a sale to any private purchaser need not be dwelt upon. The elevation of low men to the possession of power, extending even to oppression and extortion; the consequent insecurity of all previous engagements, and other evils at once occur to the mind, and attest that the practice ought not to be continued. Two other suggestions by Mr. Campbell deserve consideration. One is, that in future, if the zemindary tenure should in any case be sold to a private purchaser, materially to modify that harsh and oppressive rule, which renders voidable all engagements between the cultivators and the former zemindar. He proposes that this should be the exception instead of the rule, and that all engagements except those which should be found to have originated in collusion or fraud, should be maintained. The justice of this proposal is too obvious to require argument to enforce it, and as it would not injuriously affect any existing rights, it is difficult to discover any valid objection to it.

The

The second suggestion relates to the office of village accountant. Mr. Campbell regards it as a great error of the permanent settlement, that this office has been suffered either to fall into disuse, or to be held entirely subject to the zemindars. It was the duty of this officer, after the rates payable by the cultivators had been adjusted, to register them as the recorder of the Government, for the mutual guidance of the payers and receivers. In 1816-17, some measures were taken for the reform of the office; but Mr. Mill represents them as not having succeeded. Mr. Campbell thinks it of the highest importance that, in the permanently settled districts, it should be efficiently restored, and that the holders of it should be emancipated from the control of the zemindars, and declared the servants of Government exclusively.

Throughout a large portion of India, the inhabitants are associated in communities constituting villages, each village having its officers of different classes, and the whole community being united by various common ties. The advantages of this institution are described by Sir Charles Metcalfe with extraordinary beauty and eloquence in the following passage from one of his able minutes:

"The village communities are little republics, having nearly every thing that they want within themselves,

themselves, and almost independent of any foreign relations. They seem to last where nothing else lasts. Dynasty after dynasty tumbles down, revolution succeeds to revolution, Hindoo, Patan, Mogul, Mahratta, Siek, English, are all masters in their turn ; but the village communities remain the same. In times of trouble they arm and fortify themselves : a hostile army passes through the country : the village communities collect their cattle within their walls, and let the enemy pass unprovoked. If plunder and devastation be directed against themselves, and the force employed be irresistible, they flee to friendly villages at a distance ; but when the storm has passed over they return and resume their occupations. If a country remain for a series of years the scene of continued pillage and massacre, so that the villages cannot be inhabited, the scattered villagers nevertheless return whenever the power of peaceable possession revives. A generation may pass away ; but the succeeding generation will return. The sons will take the places of their fathers ; the same site for the village, the same positions for the houses ; the same lands will be re-occupied by the descendants of those who were driven out when the village was depopulated ; and it is not a trifling matter that will drive them out, for they will often maintain their post through times of disturbance and convulsion ; and acquire strength sufficient to resist

resist pillage and oppression with success. This union of the village communities, each one forming a separate little state in itself, has, I conceive, contributed more than any other cause to the preservation of the people of India, through all the revolutions and changes which they have suffered, and is, in a high degree, conducive to their happiness, and to the enjoyment of a great portion of freedom and independence. I wish, therefore, that the village constitutions may never be disturbed, and I dread every thing that has a tendency to break them up."

The political views embodied in the above extract are as sound as the language in which they are clothed is picturesque and forcible. A system which, through successive and protracted scenes of war and rapine, preserves the elements of property and civilization for the reconstruction of the social edifice in calmer times, has strong claims on the protection of an enlightened and paternal government; and it is gratifying to find such sentiments entertained by the statesmen of India. The principle of corporations is one admirably adapted to stability, and though a certain class of political reasoners may take a different view, the stability of social institutions will ever be regarded by the reflecting as an object which it is one of the first duties of a legislator to secure. A corporation or an associated community like an Indian village may

may be dispersed by accident; but it is not thereby destroyed. When its members come together again each man knows his place, and each man falls into it as a matter of course. The effects of a convulsion thus scarcely outlast the convulsion itself; whereas a long period must elapse, and many failures probably take place, before a number of individuals accidentally thrown together in a disorderly manner, could be formed into a tolerably regulated society.

It is not surprising that the village system of India should have been regarded as furnishing facilities for the realization of the land revenue, and that it should, in consequence, have been employed as an instrument for the purpose. The experiment has been made in various parts of India.

Through a large part of the territories under the presidency of Bombay the village system prevails, and the Government settlements are made with the head man of the village, called the potail or pateel, and some well-informed reporters bear a favourable testimony as to its success. In Madras, it failed entirely. It was introduced into the provinces under that Government about the year 1808, and the plan pursued was in consideration of a stipulated sum to be paid to Government, to surrender for a term of years the collection of the revenue to the village cultivators themselves,

themselves, or to such of them as would enter into the contract, or in the event of a general refusal to the head of the village alone. As the sum payable to Government was fixed, all advantage to be derived during the term from the extension of cultivation to waste lands was transferred to the contractors. In a few instances, the greater number of the ryots in a village joined in the lease, but generally a few only became parties to it. The result is thus stated:

"The inferior ryots were shut out from all immediate communication with the Government officers, oppressed by their more powerful brethren the renters, who in good seasons pocketed all the profits, and in bad cast upon them, by extra assessments, or saddling them with waste land, the greater burden of the leases, so that at the expiration of the ten years the village generally returned into the hands of Government in a lamentable state of impoverishment; and in some districts, particularly in Bellary, in a state, as described by Mr. Chaplin and Mr. Thackeray, of absolute bankruptcy."

It is clear that the practical result of the village system in the Madras territories, was little else than the establishment of a zemindary system under another name; and the village system of collecting the revenue appears to have a direct tendency to degenerate into this. It appears, indeed,

indeed, next to impossible to preserve it from the vices of the zemindary system; and the single advantage to be placed against this very serious disadvantage is the upholding the general system of village association. Another advantage has, indeed, been claimed for it, the collection of the revenue at a trifling expense; but it is surely better to incur some increase of expense, in order to ensure a due apportionment of the general burden, and to protect the poorer and weaker members of the community from being oppressed by the richer and stronger. If Government puts the individual ryots out of the pale of its protection, and recognizes only communities or the heads of communities, it is almost impossible but that the weak should, in many instances, receive injustice at the hands of the strong. The head of a community must occasionally have the opportunity of advancing his own interests at the expense of those of his fellow members, and it cannot be doubted that he will very frequently have the will. Even where all the cultivators in a village are parties to the contract with Government, justice cannot be regarded as secured, for communities often act with gross injustice towards individual members. In Delhi the representative of the village is chosen by the inhabitants; and though this may be viewed as a safeguard, it requires more knowledge than we possess, as to the

the mode of election and various other points, to enable us to say with confidence that jobbing is excluded, and that by this system of collection every man pays his share, and no man pays more. These observations, of course, apply only to the introduction of the village system as a general one. There may be instances where the habits of the people are so associated with it, and run so strongly in its favour, that it would be in the highest degree unwise to substitute any other. Where it already exists and works well, there it may and ought to be preserved. But it should be fully ascertained that the report of its good operation does not proceed exclusively from those who have a special interest in upholding it. The most judicious advocates of the plan propose to combine with it an individual assessment, which is, in fact, to graft it upon the ryotwar system. But the only effect of superinducing the village upon the ryotwar plan would seem to be, to ensure a just assessment, but to leave to chance the realization of a just payment. The village records, indeed, if properly kept, would afford evidence of what ought to be paid; but it is difficult to see why an aggrieved ryot should be compelled to have recourse either to a court of law or to a collector for redress, when, by the adoption of a simpler and more efficient mode of revenue administration, he might be spared the necessity of appealing to either.

either. The village institutions are most valuable, forming, as it were, the frame-work of the social system; but, except in particular cases, it will be better to place the revenue under the immediate care of the state and its servants. It is to be lamented, that in matters of taxation the consciences of men are seldom very delicate: every man endeavours to shift as much of the burden as possible from his own shoulders to those of his neighbour. It cannot be doubted that this feeling exists in India quite as strongly as in the rest of the world; and it seems reasonable that men should not be left to decide for one another where the danger of deciding unjustly is so great, but that the state should relieve them from this hazardous responsibility, and preserve to itself a power which, as between one subject and another, it has no temptation to abuse.

The great principle to be observed in any mode of settlement is, to offer as little violence as possible to the habits and feelings of the people. Wherever these do not stand in the way—wherever there is room for the exercise of a free choice, there can be no doubt at all that the ryotwar system is that which is best calculated to secure the cultivator from oppression—best calculated to promote industry, order, and independence—best calculated to advance the general prosperity of the country, and best calculated to protect the pecuniary inte-

X rests

rests of the Government. That it is generally most consonant to the feelings of the people, is certain. Mr. Sullivan relates an instance which occurred in the province of Coimbatore. The principal native officer on his establishment was rewarded for his services by a grant of revenue. The revenue had previously been paid with the utmost punctuality; but upon the grant being made to this man, the people stopped payment. The man on whom the grant had been bestowed appealed to Mr. Sullivan for assistance, to realize his claim. His interference produced an explanation of the cause of non-payment, which, it appeared, was not attributable to inability, or to any personal dislike to the individual who had obtained the grant, but solely to the aversion which the people felt to pay the Government demand through any intermediate channel. On being spoken to by Mr. Sullivan, they complained of the hardship and disgrace to which they had been subjected, in being deprived of their right to pay their revenue direct to the Government officer.

It is equally certain that the ryotwar system is the only one by which all individual rights can be protected—indeed the only one by which they can be ascertained. And thus, unless a portion of the rights of the people—probably the most valuable rights of the most valuable class of the people,

people, are to be regarded as unworthy of notice, a ryotwar settlement must be the basis of any other. Mr. Hill's observations upon this subject are much to the purpose; of course, the settlement of which he speaks is such a one as it would become a just and upright government to make. He says: "You can no more form a zemindary settlement without a ryotwar one, than you can write a correct hand without spelling, although in either case you may be unconscious of the subsidiary operation. The ryotwar settlement is an essential part of the zemindary one. If the officers of the Government do not make settlements with the ryots, the zemindar must; and therefore the objections that are taken against a ryotwar settlement will not be obviated by the substitution of the other, except in as far as those objections apply to the ryotwar settlement being executed by the officers of Government."

It is, indeed, obvious that there are but three courses that can be taken: the first is, to make an engagement for the realization of a certain revenue, without any regard to existing rights. This course no honest government can take, except in ignorance. The second is, previously to ascertain all existing rights, and then to make an engagement with an individual or a few individuals, the contracting parties being required to respect the rights which have been previously

 ascertained

ascertained and recognized. By this, all the labour and expense which by some are regarded as constituting formidable objections to the ryotwar system, are incurred in the first instance, while the benefits to be derived from them are placed in danger. The contractor may respect these rights, if he is disposed (though a conscientious contractor in India is not an every-day character), or if the holders of the rights have the means of compelling him and the inclination to use them. But why should acknowledged rights be enjoyed upon so fragile a tenure? Why, after so much time and labour have been spent in inquiring into them, should they not be placed under the immediate protection of the Government? The third course, therefore, is the only one by which the full advantages of the inquiry can be obtained—that which makes the ryotwar system, not a part of the plan adopted by Government but the whole of it; and this is the more simple, as well as the more efficacious method. It is clear, however, that when any other system is forced upon us by custom, prejudice, or any other cause, the ryotwar method must still enter into it, unless we are willing to incur the hazard of inflicting gross injustice.

The ryotwar system is the ancient one of a large part of India. Col. John Munro gives an account of it as he found it existing in Travancore, which shews its correspondence with that prevailing in the

the Company's territories. In that province it appears that a survey was made many years ago, which is the foundation of the assessment of the land revenue. Every ten or twelve years a fresh survey took place, in which alterations were made, according to the lands brought into cultivation, or those fallen into disuse. The original survey comprehended the whole of the country, whether cultivated or waste; the occasional surveys took cognizance of the cultivated lands only. Every field which yielded revenue was inserted in the survey with the name of its proprietor. It appears that a variety of tenures existed, but that no difficulties arose from this source. At the commencement of every year, an account was opened with every individual ryot; the lands he held, with their assessments, were entered, and the several payments which he made in the course of the year were also noted down, and receipts given for them. The beneficial effects of the system were, in a considerable degree, frustrated by the extreme corruption of the officers engaged in carrying it into effect. Colonel Munro says, "The system of the revenue management was so exceedingly defective, and the revenue servants were so very corrupt, that large balances of land revenue stood almost always in the accounts against the several districts, although, on examination, it was found that the ryots or the inhabitants had generally

generally paid up their rents with punctuality." With that mixture of indolence and rapacity which universally characterizes native governments, the officers appear to have been suffered to enjoy the fruits of their dishonesty for a time—but only for a time: when the Rajah's government found itself at a loss for funds, instead of demanding accounts from its unprincipled servants, it had recourse to a more ready expedient; some pretext was devised for the general confiscation of the property of these persons—an expedient which, like the zemindary system, saved trouble. No sound opinion can, of course, be formed from the practical working of any system under such a government. But from peculiar circumstances, it became necessary for the resident, Colonel Munro, to assume the direction of the internal administration, when he took the opportunity of introducing such changes as were necessary in the various departments of government; after which, the land revenue was materially improved, and the assessment generally punctually paid.

In some parts of the territories under the Bombay presidency, a modified form of the ryotwar system is adopted. The collector settles the demand against each ryot; but the collection of it is vested in the potail or head of the village. In other parts the ryotwar system exists in its pure form. It was objected by a witness before the Committee

Committee of the House of Commons in 1832, that this system was subject to two disadvantages; that " it enables the cultivator to conceal lands under cultivation without the risk of his neighbour informing against him;" and that " it enables him also, in case the Government officers are disposed to fraud, in collusion with them to diminish the revenue." These two objections are substantially one. A cultivator may, in some cases, evade the payment of a part of that which he ought to pay. This is an objection which will apply to almost every mode which human ingenuity can devise for the collection of any tax. Taxes have always been more or less evaded, and always will be. Under the zemindary system—under any system by which revenue is farmed, there may perhaps be less evasion than when it is collected by the immediate agents of Government. The chance of evading payment may be small, when the private interest of an individual is operating to quicken his vigilance in detecting the evasion. But the advantage here will be a private and not a public one. Payment will be enforced, but not for the benefit of the Government. That portion of the revenue which, in ordinary circumstances, would be withheld by the person liable to its payment, will, under a system of farming, be extracted from him only to be deposited in the pocket of the contractor; and it must be a matter of the most perfect indifference to the state, whether the sums which it ought to realize but does not, are withheld in the first instance, or whether they are intercepted in any intermediate stage. But under a vigilant and well-regulated system of revenue management, the amount lost by evasion need not be large. If care and attention be withdrawn, no system will work effectually; but if these be not wanting, that system which is least harassing to the cultivators who have to pay, will be found quite as productive as any other to the Government which has to receive.

Under the Bengal presidency, a detailed ryotwar system has been tried in Boglepoor. It was introduced in consequence of abuses arising out of the zemindary system. It was effected under the superintendence of Mr. Ward, who was deputed to that district to repress the encroachments of zemindars on lands to which they had no just claim. It is represented that Mr. Ward's arrangements have been attended with good results, and have afforded great satisfaction to the people.

But it is perhaps under the Madras presidency that the effects of the ryotwar settlement can be most justly appreciated. Between the years 1792 and 1801, we obtained from various sovereigns a vast accession of territory in this quarter.

We

We here found the ryotwar system established, and it does not appear that any other was ever known. The cultivators paid their contributions immediately into the treasury of the state, without the intervention of middle men of any kind. A part of the new territory was placed under the charge of Colonel Read. The system pursued by him proceeded upon the following principles; a settlement with each individual cultivator—the reservation to Government of the right to any increase of revenue derivable from the extension of cultivation to the waste—the fixing and recording a specific sum as *the maximum* payable on each field and each tract of unoccupied land, and where the revenue was payable in kind, the commutation into a money assessment. The surveys necessary to carry this plan into operation were executed with various degrees of care and ability, but nowhere were they so systematically and ably conducted as in the ceded districts under the superintendence of Sir Thomas Munro. The opportunity, however, of forming a judgment of the merits of the plan from actual experience, was in a great measure lost by the determination of the Government to adopt a different one, which for some reasons was supposed to be more in accordance with the judicial system then recently introduced. In consequence the ryotwar mode of settlement was abolished, except in a few districts,

tricts, and the village system substituted. It has been already seen that this entirely failed; the effect was only to introduce a zemindary system under another name, and the fate of the experiment was quickly sealed by the ruin which it occasioned. The Home Government urged the abandonment of a plan which was as much at variance with the interests of the revenue as of the community, and as soon as circumstances would admit, the local government complied. In some instances the village settlements were annulled as based in fraud; in others there had not been time to introduce them, and after a few years they every where came to a natural termination, by the expiration of the term for which they were granted. The ryotwar system was in consequence reverted to, and in the arrangements made for carrying it into effect, care was taken to guard against any errors that might formerly have been committed. The present form of the ryotwar settlement under the Madras presidency may be regarded as a modified one, inasmuch as the potail, or head of the village, is employed in its collection. The following account of the practical working of the plan will be acceptable to those who take an interest in the subject.

"In the spring of each year, every native collector, of whom there are generally ten or twelve under the European officer in charge of a large province,

province, makes the circuit of his district, to ascertain the fields which are occupied, and the individual holding the highest tenure in each. He then allows the poorer ryots to relinquish any fields they may not desire longer to retain, and grants these or other unoccupied or waste fields, to such other ryots as desire newly to extend their cultivation.

"The settlement itself is not begun by the European collector until towards the harvest, when the native collector of each district, with his district accountant, is in the first instance summoned to meet him. The records of the district accountant shew the result of the native collector's previous circuit through the villages of his district. The quantity of land in each village, with its assessment, is ascertained; that portion of it which the ryots have agreed to cultivate is distinguished from the rest, and the reduced field survey assessment on it, after the usual deductions in favour of those who have the revenue alienated to them, or remitted in their favour, forms the native collector's estimate of the probable settlement of the land revenue for the season. He then affords personal explanations as to the general state of the several villages in his district, and the local causes of those changes which are observable in the accounts compared with those of former years.

"This

"This preliminary having been completed, the village accountants are next summoned to attend the European collector. Their more detailed accounts shew how far the several ryots have completed the engagements into which they have entered with the native collector, and what fields of the land agreed to be cultivated have been left waste. The causes of these alterations are minutely investigated and explained, and the records of the village accountants are checked by information obtained from their competitors or other sources.

"The collector's native establishment then prepare from their data a separate account for every individual ryot, specifying the name of each field, whether irrigated, unirrigated, or garden-land, cultivated by him, or at his risk and charge, its number in the survey accounts, and its assessments, with the alienations, or remissions (if any) in his favour. This account also exhibits the ryot's stock, the number of his cattle, sheep, &c.; that also of the persons of his family, male or female, the extent of land exempted from revenue cultivated by him, invariably on very easy terms; and his actual payments to the Government for many years past. These, which are called the rough ryotwar accounts, form the basis of the European collector's final settlement; and when any discussion arises with a particular ryot,

ryot, they enable the collector to decide the point at issue without delay, for they contain, in fact, a summary revenue history of each individual contributor.

"These accounts having been prepared for each ryot, the whole of the cultivators themselves, in eight or ten villages, are ultimately summoned at the same time to the collector's presence. Here the account of each man, and the deductions (if any) made in his favour, are compared in detail with his own personal information by the collector's native establishment: any items in it to which objections are started, are examined, discussed, and if erroneous corrected. It is here that the frauds of the village accountants are detected, by the envy, jealousy, or honesty of one ryot pointing out the favours improperly granted to his neighbour. The objections of the ryots, if ill founded, are overruled by the explanations of the head of the village, the village accountant, or the other cultivators in the same village, or by the exhortations of the inhabitants of the neighbouring villages also present; for these persons never hesitate voluntarily to interfere, and to reprimand such as start unfounded objections; and a ryot who obstinately demurs for hours to the laboured and authoritative reasoning of the collector's native establishment, will often give way at once to the voluntary arguments of his fellows, whose

whose explanations are perhaps better adapted to his capacity, and whose opinion being more disinterested, no doubt carries with it more weight. But if the ryot's objections are valid, he always persists in appealing to the collector himself. The details of every ryotwar settlement must devolve on the native servants. The presence of the European officer is, no doubt, useful to superintend the whole; but it is chiefly requisite, in order to afford, on the spot, to every discontented ryot, this facility of instant access and immediate appeals, which affords the best check against either fraud or oppression in the course of the settlement. The collector, if a judicious revenue officer, seldom has occasion to decide such questions himself; he soon learns to distinguish amongst the ryots assembled, which are those universally respected throughout the country for their good conduct, impartiality, and sound sense; and his call upon them for an opinion, invariably given publicly without any previous preparation, whilst it silences all complaint, relieves the officer of the Government from the odium of deciding questions in which its interests may often be involved.

"All discussions with the ryots having thus been terminated, the puttah or lease, and its counterpart, are drawn out, and the former having been sealed by the collector, the whole of the ryots in each village are called before him. Every man here

here separately exchanges engagements with the Government, to the number of 60,000 or 70,000 in some provinces, and receives from the European collector's own hands his lease, accompanied by the betel leaf, &c., the usual seal of all native compacts. If any ryot still objects to the terms of his lease, he declines to receive it, and the grounds of his objection are here formally discussed, and finally decided by the collector in open public audience.

"In each village its head or potail, the chief of the police, is also invariably the village collector on account of Government. He realizes from each individual ryot the amount of the government revenue as the instalments fall due, and remits it to the native collector of the district, also vested with magisterial powers similar to those of a justice of the peace, whence it is forwarded to the European collector, uniting in his person the superintendence of both the revenue and police departments over the entire province."

Such is the mode of proceeding adopted in those parts of the territories under the Madras presidency subject to the ryotwar system, and it appears to possess many advantages. Among the most important may be reckoned the intercourse which it ensures between the European servant of the Government and the contributors to the revenue, and the publicity which attends this intercourse.

course. It may be doubted, however, whether there may not be danger, that deference to the individual opinion of natives may be carried somewhat too far. The points which arise for determination must, indeed, generally be such as a stranger in the country, however acute, accomplished, and laborious, must be less competent to decide than natives, if integrity be secured; but the state of Indian society is so universally corrupt, that it can be scarcely possible to obtain an honest opinion, even where there is no apparent motive to dishonesty. At the same time, it is not possible to devise a system better calculated to elicit the truth than to hear all that can be said; but the collector, after all, should not attach too much importance to the testimony or the opinion of any individual, but exercise his discrimination, in endeavouring to extract the truth from the discordant statements with which he is assailed.

The ryotwar system is applicable to any part of India where custom, prejudice, or positive law does not exclude it. Where different tenures exist, the settlement should be made with the holder of the highest, but he should be required to produce satisfactory evidence of his right. Where lands are cultivated by several ryots in common, on equal joint co-tenure, the names of all should be inserted in the lease, and the share held

held by each distinctly specified. The claims upon the revenue itself can occasion no difficulty, except in ascertaining them. When ascertained, if the claim be to a partial remission, it will be admitted in the settlement; if to a total exemption, there will be no occasion for any settlement at all.

The objections which have been urged against the ryotwar system are principally two: that it subverts the established order of society by reducing all classes to the lowest level, and that it is more expensive than any other system for the administration of the land revenue. The first is obviously groundless. The system recognizes all existing rights, and protects them all in their proper order. It does not, like the zemindary system, create rights which never existed, and sacrifice all old rights to the new. The highest tenant of the Government, whoever he may be, and by whatever name distinguished, is admitted to settlement; and if there are a number holding equal rights in common, they are all admitted. So far, therefore, from subverting the established order of society, the system preserves every man in his proper place; and instead of levelling, it upholds all distinctions which it finds in existence.

The objection, based on the alleged increase of expense, is more plausible, but equally fallacious. Under the ryotwar system, the expense of realizing the

the revenue stands prominently forward, without disguise or concealment. Under the zemindary and village systems, the actual sacrifice on the part of Government is placed out of sight. In the Bengal settlement the Government supposed that it was paying for the collection of the revenue about ten or fifteen per cent. It is now actually paying about one hundred per cent.; and though a portion of this is undoubtedly derived from extortion, yet some considerable part might, under a better system, have been appropriated by Government without doing wrong to the cultivators. Under the zemindary system the *net* amount, after these monstrous deductions, appears as the *gross* amount of the land revenue, and the trifling sum necessary for the remaining establishments of Government appears as the entire charge of collection. The village system, in proportion as it approaches the zemindary, partakes of its evils and its fallacies. Whereas, by the ryotwar settlement, while the entire sum raised from the land appears as revenue, the amount is subject to the deduction of the entire expense of collection, which appears as undisguised as that on which it is a charge. To compare systems so different, in the sweeping manner in which the comparison is sometimes made, is obviously most unfair. Mr. Lewin, whose experience referred to Malabar and Canara, in answer to the question, "Is the collection of the

the revenue, under the ryotwar system, very expensive in detail?" answered, " No, I think not; very cheap, I should imagine. I believe it is calculated at five per cent., or not even so much; but it would be extremely difficult to make a correct calculation, because the revenue officers and the police officers perform the same duty." This calculation may not, in all cases, be borne out by fact; but if the charges exceed five per cent., there is no reason to believe that they reach the *estimated* zemindary profit of fifteen per cent., and it is beyond the possibility of doubt, that they cannot be placed in comparison with the *actual* zemindary profit of a hundred per cent. If the two systems are to be compared in point of expense, they ought to be compared fairly; and if they are, the overwhelming advantages of the ryotwar settlement will be evident. Yet, after all, the question of expense is a secondary one: it is subordinate to those which refer to the maintenance of ancient rights, the promotion of general prosperity, and the securing justice to all, by constant and vigilant European superintendence. If the expense of the ryotwar system were somewhat greater than that of the zemindary, instead of being almost incredibly less, it would still deserve to be preferred, on account of its beneficial effects.

Of all the modes of realizing a revenue from land, the ryotwar is the best, and land must doubtlessly

 continue

continue to be the great source of revenue in India. A good deal of discussion has taken place on the nature of the Government claim upon the land—whether it ought to be regarded in the character of a rent or of a tax. The question is not perhaps of any great importance—certainly of no practical importance. Political economists may split hairs in determining the precise limit between two payments, the effects of which upon the payer are precisely similar; but though their intellectual ingenuity may be highly gratifying to themselves, the probability of its being beneficial to mankind is small indeed. The claim of Government upon the land of India appears certainly strongly to resemble rent; but a land-tax in any country must bear the same resemblance. If in England, or any country under similar circumstances, the Government were to impose a very small additional charge upon the land, it is possible that the occupier would pay it out of his profits. But if the charge were a heavy one this would be impossible, and it would operate to diminish the landlord's rent. The claim of Government would thus operate precisely like the claim of a mortgagee, or any other incumbrancer of landed property. The more he took the less would there be for the landlord; and it is possible to conceive the amount of the demand of Government increased until the right of the landlord would

would be worth nothing. The answer given by a very ingenious and able writer, to a question proposed under the authority of the Board of Control, does not appear perfectly satisfactory. The question asks, " How far the land revenue, whether received by Government or through an intermediate person, resembles or differs from the rent of land, or resembles or differs from a tax imposed by law ?" and the answer is, that " the land revenue in India, as generally assessed, differs from rent only in respect to amount, according as it is less or more than what exists after the cost of cultivation is replaced." It is added, that " when a fixed proportion of the produce was taken as revenue, it was a tax of the nature of tythe in England." Now it seems extraordinary that a payment in kind should be a tax, and that the commutation of the charge into money should convert it into rent. Notwithstanding tythe is adverted to as invariably a tax, yet when commuted, upon the principle laid down, it becomes rent. In many parts of the world the landlords receive their revenue in kind; because from local causes they can obtain it in no other way. In this case, upon the principle just quoted, these persons would not draw rent, but impose a tax. It would seem more correct to regard the cultivator and landlord as partners; the former bringing to the partnership his labour and his capital

when

when he has any, though where such a system prevails, the cultivator is often so poor that the landlord is obliged to advance seed to sow the ground. The landlord brings to the partnership his land, and the profits of the enterprize are divided according to a given arrangement. The introduction of a money payment relieves the landlord from trouble, and secures him, in some degree, from the risk of loss arising from bad management; and it gives to the occupier the advantage of all the profit which he can make upon the landlord's share beyond the stipulated payment. Such an arrangement is therefore generally beneficial to all the parties interested. It is beneficial in the case of tythe as in any other; but it is not more so, the main difference between the claim of the tythe-holder and the claim of the landlord, being that the former is limited by law, and the latter is not. The tythe-holder, in fact, to the extent of his right, stands in the place of a landlord, and whatever might be taken from the claimant of the tenth part, would be transferred to the pocket of the claimant of the other nine. The mere renter of land will, in ordinary cases, never obtain more than the price of his labour, and a fair interest for the capital which he invests. The surplus produce, either in money or in kind, will pass into other hands, and to him individually it matters nothing, whether into the hands

hands of a Government collector, of a landlord, or of a tythe-holder, whether it be divided between two of them or distributed among all three. Upon principles of state policy, the question may be worth discussing, but not as respects the individual cultivator, whose only interest is to avoid paying too much. Between rent and a tax upon land, therefore, there is no difference but in name. The two charges are exactly alike, and resemble several others which pass by different names. Where there is but one species of claim upon the land, the surplus produce flows into a single channel—where there are two or more it is divided.

The really important question for the Indian cultivator is as to the amount of his assessment. If that be moderate, he may feel perfectly unconcerned whether it is called by one name or another. That it should be moderate, is desirable, not more for his individual benefit, than for the general prosperity of the community. An extravagant assessment, like an exorbitant rent, will rarely be realized; and it needs no argument to shew that a body of insolvent cultivators is inconsistent with national prosperity. If they are kept one step above this state—just able to defray the demands of the Government, but enjoying little and accumulating nothing—the best that can be looked for will be that the

country

country should be stationary. But it is not desirable that any country should remain stationary; and India, especially, is yet too far removed from a state of general prosperity to allow her to take her station where she is, and decline to advance further. The ryots are said to be generally improvident, but nothing makes men so improvident as extreme misery. By improving their condition, we shall impart to them the desire of improving it still further. By enabling them to acquire property, we shall give them the means of effecting improvements and extending the productive powers of the soil. By giving them the power and the inclination to consume, we shall afford a stimulus to manufacturing and commercial industry, and thus increase the means of employment and multiply the resources of the country. By leaving in the hands of the ryot some portion of the surplus produce of the land, we shall elevate his character, and in time perhaps call into existence such a class of men as the permanent zemindary system was intended to create, but failed of creating—men deriving an income from the land, and in consequence acquiring a certain place in society. The ryot "cultivating his own," has a claim to this at our hands. He has a heritable interest in the soil—his title is much more ancient than ours, and has survived through every variety of change and convulsion.

convulsion. Justice and policy coincide in requiring that he should be treated with liberality.

The evils of over-assessment are of course greater in India, where few of the cultivators possess any capital, than they would be in a country differently situated in this respect. In any country it would produce considerable distress. In India its effect must generally be utter ruin and destitution ; and as the evils are greater, so the danger of incurring them is more imminent. In England, not only do landlords sometimes demand too much, but tenants agree to pay it, notwithstanding the latter have always some capital, and to a considerable extent a choice of farms. In India the cultivator holds himself attached to the land which his forefathers have cultivated for many generations, and rather than forego the possession of it, he will be tempted into engagements which it is impossible for him to fulfil. As such engagements must end in disappointment on the one side and ruin on the other, it is clearly for the benefit of both parties that they should not be formed. But the only effectual preventive will be moderation on the part of Government. More must not be demanded than is reasonable, or the consequence will be that less will be obtained. We must not indulge the fallacious belief, that by increasing our assessments we shall insure a proportionate

increase

increase of our receipts. Swift has observed, that in political arithmetic two and two do not always make four, and this is not less true now than it was in his day, and certainly not less applicable to India than to all other countries. Some disappointment will, under any assessment, continue to be experienced in realizing the claims of Government upon the small ryots; property from the injurious laws of succession being frequently divided into such minute portions as to render the payment of any revenue scarcely possible. The cause of this evil is of too delicate a nature to be hastily dealt with, and it is probably one of those inconveniences to which we must be content, for a time at least, to submit.

Colonel Colebrook suggested the redemption of the land revenue as a measure calculated to benefit the people; and he stated that in Ceylon the system had been in operation for ten or twelve years past with good effect, the people in some provinces having been allowed to redeem the whole of their rents above a tenth. He added, that the returns from those districts shewed that the revenue had increased rather than diminished, notwithstanding the redemption of the assessment, a tenth being now as productive as a fourth or a third formerly was, an effect which he ascribes to new land being brought into cultivation. Captain Duff recommends a similar measure,

measure, and there can be little room for difference of opinion as to its advantages. But it is quite clear that, however desirable, it cannot be effected without capital, and Indian cultivators have for the most part no capital. When they have amassed any (and by a judicious course of proceeding on the part of Government that time may arrive,) the subject may be revived, and its details will then become interesting matter of enquiry. One point is clear—the redemption must be effected by the ryot, or the association of ryots who claim right in the land. A stranger must not be permitted to redeem the revenue, as such a permission would introduce all the evils of the permanent zemindary system under another form.

The redemption of the land revenue at present calls for no minute consideration. But what are our prospects as to the revenue itself, is a question of immediate and pressing interest. Of late years there has been a slight improvement in the revenue derived from the lower provinces of the Bengal presidency—but for the permanent settlement there would have been a very great one, as has occurred in the western provinces. In the Madras and Bombay territories the revenue has declined, owing to fall of prices, unfavourable seasons, and other causes. There has, indeed, been a general fall of prices throughout the East; but

but this can scarcely be regarded as remarkable, seeing that the same effect has been taking place throughout the world. As has been observed, it is in the provinces under the Madras and Bombay presidencies that the evil has been most severely felt. The evidence which has been brought forward on the subject throws little light upon the matter, and the speculations of political economists cannot be expected to throw much more. The witnesses whose evidence bears most directly upon the point are Lieut.-Col. Barnewall and Lieut.-Col. Sykes, both highly intelligent men. The former, in answer to the question, "To what circumstances do you attribute the fall in value of agricultural produce?" says, "To the altered condition of the country, and to the large establishments maintained by the Guicowar government and other states being reduced. This has caused a less demand, while a state of internal peace prevents all extra demand. Nearly the whole of the population has become agricultural, and the supply of grain so far exceeds the consumption, that there had been a glut in all the markets for one or two years in the provinces on the western side of India before I left it. The effects of importations of cotton cloths from England had greatly lowered manufactures, and commerce was also languid." The coincidence between this state of of things and that which has occurred at home is striking. The reduction of establishments and a state of universal peace have been attended with the same results in India as here. This process political economists have often undertaken to explain, but have never yet succeeded. Its existence is, indeed, a bitter satire on the prevailing systems ; as, according to them, the state described ought to be one of extraordinary prosperity. The destruction of the home manufacture of cotton cloths ought not, on the same principles, to create any inconvenience ; yet it evidently appears to sensible and unprejudiced observers to be one of the elements of the mass of misery. The fact is, in spite of the assertions of the fashionable school of political economy, that a period of transition from high to low prices is always a period of general and intense suffering. Colonel Sykes appears at a loss to account for the great fall of prices; and he admits it—unlike the spinners of cobweb systems of political economy, who profess to be ignorant of nothing. Colonel Sykes's attention was called to a statement of Sir John Malcolm, in his account of Central India, "that the sudden cessation of war, and the return of the population to peaceful habits and the cultivation of the land, had both diminished the number of consumers and greatly increased the number of producers," to which Sir John attributed a very remarkable

remarkable fall in prices in certain provinces; and Colonel Sykes was asked, "Can the fall of prices in the Deccan be attributed to a similar cause?" He answers, that if such were the cause, there would necessarily appear a much larger extent of cultivation upon the returns than formerly, but that, on the contrary, the breadth of cultivation had diminished. This is an extraordinary fact, and it ought to be mentioned, that Colonel Sykes's opinion is the result, not of a random guess, but of a deliberate inquiry. It is probable, that one part of the theory of Sir John Malcolm is applicable to the case—the number of producers is not increased, but the number of consumers is diminished. To exist, men must consume agricultural produce, more or less, but a very small consumption will sustain life; and if from any cause a large portion of the people are compelled to reduce their consumption to the lowest degree, it requires not the taper of philosophy to shew that the producers must suffer. The land goes out of cultivation because the produce cannot be sold; yet there are vast numbers who would be glad to purchase, but they want the money. The cultivator finds it difficult to sell enough to procure a sufficiency to supply his own necessities and to meet the claims of Government, and in many cases he finds it impossible; while the consumer, or he who ought to be a consumer, perishes for

want,

want, or prolongs a wretched existence upon an insufficient supply of that food which the producer cannot sell, and therefore discontinues to raise. Whatever may be the cause of this unhappy state of things, it cannot, at all events, without the most palpable folly, be ascribed to "the pressure of population against the supply of food."

It is generally difficult, and often impossible, to trace with accuracy the precise causes of national distress. The most fatal mistakes are in consequence committed, and remedies are applied which aggravate instead of abating the evil. The diseases which assail the springs of national prosperity require to be treated with extraordinary caution. Nostrums for removing them always abound; but their alleged virtues should be very strictly scrutinized before they are adopted. In our own country, from the period of the termination of the war, we have been continually trying experiments for the removal of the distress which followed that event, and they have all failed. We are therefore entitled to conclude, that all we have hitherto done is wrong, though what is right is by no means so apparent. In India, the state of things being much less complicated and artificial than here, we might suppose that the same degree of difficulty would not be found, yet we are, in truth, nearly as much in the dark with regard to the distress existing in that country, as to that

that which we have to lament in our own. There are one or two leading principles which we may adopt with a pretty strong confidence that we are right; and at present, perhaps, neither practical experience nor theoretical speculation can help us beyond them.

In the first place, the assessment on the land, as has already been recommended, should be moderate. It must be conformed, in some degree, to the altered circumstances of the times, and the motives to such a course, arising from its justice and policy, are corroborated by the obvious impossibility of succeeding in a contrary one. The amount of receipt must clearly be limited by the capacity to pay, and an attempt to extract too much will defeat its own object, and end in disappointment, ruin the cultivator, and throw still more land into waste. Moderation in the claims of Government is therefore indispensable, and care should be taken, not only that the State does not press injuriously upon the subject, but, as far as possible, that those persons who stand between the State and the subject do not promote their personal interests at the expense of both.

It seems tolerably certain also, that in the present state of India, the advice of those authorities in economical science, who recommend giving a stimulus to consumption rather than to production, is the sounder and more beneficial. The desire

desire to consume is, of course, vain without the power to acquire. But in a country where land is sufficient and labour abundant, the power should not be wanting. The great impediment to an increased consumption of European goods in India is the difficulty of procuring a return. The interests of Europe and Asia are thus identical, and an increased demand in the West for the commodities of the East, would be equally beneficial to both parts of the world. To promote this, all duties which press heavily and unequally on the produce of East-Indian industry should be abolished. Our fellow-subjects in one part of the globe should not be sacrificed to our fellow-subjects in another, nor even to those at home; still less ought they to be sacrificed to strangers. Called, as we have been, to administer the government of a populous and mighty empire, with which we have no natural connexion, it is a solemn duty to exercise the extraordinary power we have acquired, so as to advance the best interests of the people over whom we rule. We must regard them not as aliens, but as countrymen, separated from us by distance, but entitled to receive the same degree of consideration, and the same impartial protection from the Supreme Government as ourselves. Whatever commercial advantages are enjoyed by their competitors, either at home or in the colonies, should be conceded to them. If the one class is subject to taxation, the other should be subject to it also in the same, but not in a greater degree. If the industry of one is favoured by protection, so should that of the other. The different circumstances existing in different parts of the same empire, may require variations in the laws; but commercial jealousies, and commercial inequalities arising out of those jealousies, must not be tolerated among fellow-subjects. To remove them is an act not of grace and favour, but of justice.

There are some internal charges upon trade which operate as discouragements to consumption, and which should therefore be abolished as soon as the state of the revenue will appear to justify it. The transit duties are both injurious and vexatious; and since they are eminently fertile in fraud and chicane, their abolition would be as beneficial to morality as to commerce.

As the decline in the revenue has not hitherto been great, and as the deficiency in one part of our territories has been made up in another, there is every reason to hope that, by a moderate assessment, and a judicious financial system, *aided by the concession on the part of the United Kingdom of the just claims* of India, any permanent diminution of revenue may be averted; that prosperity may revive in those provinces where it has declined; the land again be brought into cultivation, and the people

people placed in circumstances of ease and contentment. From the introduction of European capital, skill, and enterprize, much may be expected. Their beneficial effects will not be confined to the parts of India open to European residents; they will be extended to all in a greater or less degree.

It is scarcely necessary to point out how closely the prosperity of India is connected with that of England. In the present advanced state of commercial intercourse, prices have a tendency to equalize themselves all over the world, and a rise or fall in one country, will almost invariably act upon every other. Consequently, whatever acts beneficially upon the great interests of England, will have the same effect upon India, which partaking in the prosperity of the protecting country, will repay the benefit with ample interest.

The subject of currency is a delicate one; but in seeking for the probable causes of the decline of prices, it is impossible to exclude its consideration. In the Deccan, the facts connected with this branch of enquiry (as stated by Colonel Sykes) appear so anomalous and extraordinary, as to defy all attempts at reasoning upon them. In the Western Provinces, Mr. Mackenzie appears disposed to regard the fall of prices as owing to a diminished supply of silver. This might arise from various causes; and it is a question of some

 interest,

interest, how far the state of other countries has, in this respect, operated upon India.

The quantity of the precious metals possessed by any country must be influenced by various other causes besides the will of the Government. The nature of the circulating medium, and the state of the coinage, are matters of purely legislative arrangement. In India, the rupee, as is well known, is the coin in which accounts are kept, and which is the principal medium of exchange; but rupees of different values circulate in the different provinces, and the propriety of continuing these varieties, or putting an end to them by the establishment of a uniform currency, has been of late much discussed. A few observations on the subject may not be misplaced in the present chapter.

The rupees current within the territories included under the old Bengal presidency, are two, the Calcutta sicca rupee, and the Furruckabad rupee; the standard of both is the same; but the sicca rupee weighs about 192 grains troy (176 silver); the Furruckabad 180 grains (165 silver). In the Madras and Bombay territories, the rupee in circulation corresponds very nearly, if not entirely, with the Furruckabad rupee. There is another description of rupee which, though now an ideal coin, must be noticed, because it is still recognized in military accounts. Previously to the

the regulations by which the present currency of Bengal was established, the rupees were distinguished by the year in which they were struck. After circulating for a few years they became depreciated, whether they had lost weight or not, and were reckoned sonat rupees, or rupees of years. To put an end to this, it was determined that in future all rupees should bear the same date; but, for reasons the validity of which it is unnecessary to discuss, the pay of the Bengal troops continued to be reckoned in the Sonat, or depreciated rupee.

The circulation of the rupee of each presidency is confined to the territories subject to it. In all other places it is received only as bullion; and, except at the mints, is not a legal tender. To obviate these inconveniences, it has been proposed to establish a uniform coinage throughout the British dominions in India. Nothing would have a greater tendency to facilitate commercial operations; and whatever has this effect, tends to the advancement of a nation in wealth and prosperity. Now that the whole of our Indian possessions have, for legislative purposes, been placed under one government, the proper time for establishing a uniformity of coinage seems to have arrived. It would be thought a strange arrangement, if one species of coin circulated exclusively in the English counties north of the Trent, another in in the counties south of that river, and a third in Wales—if the silver coin, which commanded every species of commodity at Bristol, should become useless to the traveller on his arrival at Cardiff, and he should consequently be subjected to the inconvenience of seeking out a money-changer, and to the loss arising from the transaction which would be necessary to enable him to obtain a supply of the necessaries of life. Custom only can reconcile us to a similar state of things in India.

If the currency be rendered uniform, as it ought to be, a question arises as to the value of the circulating rupee. It has been urged that the Madras rupee is the most extensively circulated, and that the new coin should be equivalent to it. The propriety of this decision has been questioned by a very eminent authority, who asks why the sicca rupee should not be adopted. In support of this it is urged, that the public debt is contracted in the sicca rupee; that the sicca rupee is the coin of the settled territory, where the introduction of any other would subject Government to the alternative of either sustaining a serious loss, by receiving its revenue in a coin nominally the same, but actually of inferior value; or of committing an *apparent* breach of faith, by demanding from the zemindars a larger number of rupees than they had been accustomed to pay, and thus also unsettling all existing contracts between them

and

and the ryots; that the sicca rupee is the established currency of the most opulent and most commercial portion of our Indian possessions; and that, within a period of thirty years, nearly as great an amount has been coined and issued of the sicca rupee as of all the other coins of British India taken collectively. These points demand serious consideration; and they would almost seem to determine the question in favour of the sicca rupee, especially as it does not appear that any inconvenience could arise from its introduction into the Madras and Bombay territories. In these, instead of nominally increasing the assessment, the Government would have the more gracious task of making an apparent reduction. In other respects, the operation in those provinces, as far as any effect at all would be produced, would be beneficial. Under either plan, some small difficulty might arise in the payment of the army—and this is a matter not to be tampered with. It has been stated, that in Bengal the pay of the troops is reckoned in the sonat or depreciated rupee; but it is, of course, issued in the sicca rupee, calculated at the rate of 104½ sonat to 100 sicca. If the sicca rupee were adopted for general circulation, the old system might be preserved. If the Madras rupee were preferred, as that is about 6½ per cent. inferior to the sicca, while the sonat is calculated at only 4½, this difference must

must be noticed and accounted for. Here, however, a real difficulty occurs. It has been suggested, that if we give the Bengal army the advantage of the 2 per cent. difference between the value of the sonat and the Madras rupee, the troops of the other presidencies would expect the same. And this seems an addditional reason for preferring the sicca rupee; for though the troops of Madras and Bombay might feel some disappointment at receiving a smaller number of rupees than heretofore, yet the same thing must have occurred to the Bengal troops when the new rupee was substituted for the old depreciated one; and the difficulty might, perhaps, be surmounted in the same way, by keeping the accounts according to the Madras and Bombay rupee, and making payment in the sicca. The sonat rupee being regarded as equivalent to that of Furruckabad, and this latter differing little in value from the rupees of Madras and Bombay, the Bengal troops would have an advantage—but this they have now. Whether or not they ought to retain it—whether the advantage should be withdrawn from them or extended to the other presidencies—or whether they should, in this respect, remain precisely as at present, are questions open to discussion, but which do not affect that relating to a uniform currency. The evils arising from the present complexity of coins and currency have been felt and lamented

lamented by military men, among whom may be mentioned Sir Robert Scott and Sir Henry Worsley.

It has been proposed to extend the uniformity of coinage to gold and copper; and though of less importance, this seems a necessary consequence of establishing a uniform silver currency. The sicca rupee appears, on the whole, the best adapted for the latter purpose, and it has the additional advantage of a very near approach to that of Great Britain. This has been pointed out by Mr. St. George Tucker, and he has suggested that the assimilation might be made complete, and the sicca rupee, by a very slight alteration, converted into a two-shilling piece, it now exceeding two shillings only by the fraction D. 566.

CHAPTER XII.

MEANS OF SECURING BRITISH INTERESTS AND AUTHORITY.

THE British entered India as traders. They were compelled to exchange the operations of commerce for the labours of war. Success attended their military career, and renewed provocations urged them to continue it. Victory has followed victory, and conquest been accumulated upon conquest, until the dominion of Britain embraces the larger portion of India, and its influence extends over the whole. To look back upon the achievements of our countrymen, cannot but be gratifying to our national sympathies; to look forward to the probable fate of that empire, which their skill and courage raised from such small beginnings, is a duty which is imposed upon us by a regard to our national honour, as well as to the integrity of the British dominions.

The stability and permanency of our power may be endangered either from within or from without. Our first attention must naturally be directed to our own subjects. From their hostility, if provoked, our greatest danger would arise; on their attachment,

attachment, if secured, our safety may be firmly based. To acquire the confidence of the people over whom we rule, and having acquired, to preserve it, must be the grand objects of our policy. The only way to effect these desirable objects, is to place the people as much as possible at their ease. A nation naturally judges of its government by the degree of good which it enjoys under its sway, and appears to derive from it. The majority of every nation, too, regard principally the time that is passing over their heads, and are little disposed to sacrifice present to prospective advantages. From this caüse, all changes of which the inconveniences are immediate, and the benefits remote, are unpopular, and nowhere more so than among a people like that of India, constitutionally averse to change. When the inconvenience, which is to be the price of the alleged improvement, is certain, while the benefit is contingent, the dislike will be greatly increased; and if the mighty fabric of British dominion in the East should either prematurely moulder away or fall with a sudden shock, its decline or destruction will probably originate in rash and injudicious attempts to introduce a state of things presumed to be better than that existing, but for which the natives are unprepared, and which consequently, instead of being a step in advance will in effect be a step backward. In

India

India we must leave European prejudices behind us, if we would retain possession of the country; and while our most anxious thoughts and our most strenuous exertions are devoted to the promotion of its substantial interests, we must lay aside that mania for improvement, which in the West is not unattended with evil, and in the East must be regarded as the sure precursor of convulsion and ruin. Prudence is not less necessary than good intention. The improvement of the state of the people must be effected in their own way if it be effected at all. Enthusiastic politicians will endeavour to effect this at once, and they will undervalue the silent, but certain operation of time: yet time is one of the most powerful agents in forming the character and fixing the destinies of nations. Its effect is strikingly exemplified in British India. In those parts which have been longest subjected to our rule, our power is most firmly established. The people and the government have become more habituated to each other, and our authority is more cheerfully recognized from a perception of the benefits which it has conferred.

One element of security will be found, in the exchange of habits of war and rapine, for the cultivation of the arts of peace; and in proportion as we protect and advance the interests of agricultural, commercial, and manufacturing industry,

try, shall we promote the stability of our rule. The military adventurer may expect to benefit by a state of tumult and anarchy; but from such a state the industrious classes have nothing to hope, and every thing to dread. To give industry a fair field for exertion, is then to uphold the existing authority; and this is a consideration well worthy the attention of the Legislature of Great Britain, who, alone, have the power of removing from the industry of India the burdens which at present bear it down.

But while the arts of peace are treated with favour, we must be prepared for the opposite state if it should become necessary. Looking to this contingency, the Indian army becomes an object of vast importance. It has been said, that our dominion in India has been gained by the sword, and that it must be maintained by the sword. The first of these propositions it will be needless to discuss; the second cannot be admitted without some qualification. If our dominion were merely that of the sword, its tenure could not be regarded as otherwise than very uncertain, inasmuch as the sword, though wielded at our command, is substantially in the hands of those whom we are to coerce. The same view seems to have dictated the opinion, that we are in a situation unparalleled in the history of the world—retaining possession of a conquered country by means of a native army. But

But it is wrong to suppose that our dominion depends solely upon the army. Many governments have been established by force; but few have ever maintained their dominion by such means. Still less do governments rest upon the phantom "public opinion." Governments for the most part exist, because they have been accustomed to exist. When the people are rendered happy, they are, undoubtedly, more secure; but obedience is more the result of habit than of any thing else. An old government, unless very feeble or very oppressive, is generally pretty secure, and every year may thus be regarded as adding something to the strength of ours in India. But no government can afford to be despised, and with such an extent of territory as we possess, a large portion of it being of very recent acquisition, and in the midst of a people among whom we are comparatively strangers, a numerous and effective army cannot be spared. Our dominions are not assailable from without only. Within their circle are portions of territory under the rule of native powers—nominally allies, indeed, but for the most part, to be regarded as hollow friends. The formidable alliance formed some years since to drive us from India, shews the feelings with which we are regarded by the old Mahometan authorities; and though their power is now broken and destroyed, we must not imagine that their

hostile

hostile feeling towards us is abated. We must, therefore, at all times be prepared to defend ourselves. The knowledge that we are so prepared will be the best security for our safety and the general peace. With regard to those states, there can be little reason to doubt that our influence over them must be that of fear. It is important, therefore, to ascertain how far our native troops are to be depended upon. In this respect, the very absence of the loftier qualities of the military character may be considered to be in our favour. To the love of country—to those high and chivalric feelings of loyalty and patriotism which elevate the soldier into the hero, they are strangers. They are undoubtedly pure mercenaries, and would as readily fight for one master as for another. We have consequently nothing to apprehend from the operation of feelings which do not exist; and we must not conclude, that because they are deficient in the more graceful and noble characteristics, they are therefore wanting in the coarser qualifications of the military character. They have generally behaved well in the field; and, like other soldiers of fortune, their fidelity may be relied on as long as we make their interest coincident with it. The importance of securing this is manifest; and, on the whole, the adherence of the native soldier may be commanded with tolerable ease. He serves for pay, and his pay should

be

be good, and discharged with as much regularity as possible. Like all his countrymen, he is under the influence of deep prejudices, and his prejudices must not be treated with insult. Though mercenary and prejudiced, he is docile and obedient, especially under mild treatment; and he should, therefore; meet from the European authorities generally, and from his officers in particular, consideration and kindness. The habits of military life naturally beget an attachment between the soldier and his officer, unless there be great faults on one side, or on both. The manner in which European officers have spoken of the sepoys, and the attachment which, in some instances, the latter have shewn for their officers, prove that the feelings which are so desirable for the benefit of the service, may exist in an army constituted like that of India.

We may conclude, then, that our Indian army would be found efficient against an enemy either from within or from without. Happily, there is but little probability of their being tried against either. Our old antagonist, France, is not in a condition to contest with us the dominion of the East, and it must be long before her circumstances so far alter as to enable her to enter into such a contest with any prospect of success. From other quarters there is nearly as little to apprehend. The frontier of our dominions is singularly

singularly unassailable, considering the extent of territory; the country, of which a part is subjected to our direct rule, and the whole to our influence, being in a great degree secured by nature from external attack. The sea rolls around a large portion of it; mountains, affording few passes, and desert countries scarcely passable at all, bound the rest. Russia has been regarded with some apprehension, and she may possibly be well disposed to add India to her vast empire; but Russia would perhaps find it no easy task to transport and maintain the vast armies which would be necessary to give even a chance of success. It would occupy too much space to enter into a discussion of the various routes which might be adopted, and of the facilities afforded by each. The friendship of Persia, if not indispensable to our security, is at least an auxiliary to it, and with that country our relations are altogether amicable. A minister has long resided there accredited by the Indian Government; but either from the importance of the mission, or from some other cause, his place is in future to be supplied by one appointed directly by the British crown. But, at present, we need not Persia to stand between Russia and India. Russia has quite enough to occupy all her energy and all her capacity for intrigue in a quarter more dear to her ambition than India. The incorporation of

 Turkey

Turkey with her dominions, is now the object to which she is willing to sacrifice every other. This achieved, she might turn her eyes further eastward. At present, however, it is gratifying to know that the British empire in India is in such a state of security, as must disarm every fear, and leave its rulers at perfect liberty to devote an undivided attention to the advancement of the happiness of the people.

THE END.